D0269265

Curtains and Blinds

**TRICKS OF
THE TRADE**

Curtains and Blinds

HELEN O'LEARY

PELHAM BOOKS

First published in Great Britain by
PELHAM BOOKS LTD
44 Bedford Square
London WC1B 3DU
1982

Copyright © Helen O'Leary 1982

All Rights Reserved. No part of this publication may be reproduced,
stored in a retrieval system, or transmitted, in any form or by any
means, electronic, mechanical, photocopying, recording or otherwise,
without the prior permission of the Copyright owner.

British Library Cataloguing in Publication Data
O'Leary, Helen
    Curtains and blinds. — (Tricks of the trade)
    1. Curtain making   2. Blinds.
    I. Title   II. Series
    646.2'1   TT390

ISBN 0 7207 1419 2

Typeset by Cambrian Typesetters, Farnborough, Hants.
Printed in Great Britain by Hollen Street Press Ltd, Slough,
and bound by Robert Hartnoll Ltd, Bodmin.

Contents

Metric/Imperial Conversion Table

All soft-furnishing fabrics are sold by the metre these days and their width is given in centimetres, but here's a quick conversion table for the measurements used in this book, just in case you still think in inches. In some cases the equivalent given is only an approximate figure.

2.5 cm = 1 in.
7.5 cm = 3 in.
10 cm = 4 in.
15 cm = 6 in.

1 m = 39½ in. approx.
122 cm = 48 in.
137 cm = 54 in.
183 cm = 72 in.

Introduction

The trouble with making your own curtains is getting started — never mind needing the ability to achieve satisfactory results! Measuring up windows, estimating fabric requirements, not to mention cutting out mounds of material, can be a terrifying task for most of us. While having to estimate fabric requirements in metric widths only adds to the general fear and confusion.

Yet no special sewing skills are needed to make successful curtains. What you do need to know, however, are the professional curtain maker's shortcuts and quick ways to simplify and speed up the process. So read on: help is at hand.

The aim of this book is to pass on to you these professional 'tricks of the trade'; to remove some of the stress and strain, and help you make stunning curtains. In the following pages every aspect of window treatment is discussed: the fixtures and fittings you will need to provide a professional finish; the best and easiest way to make up lined and unlined curtains; how to use commercial heading tapes effectively and how to work individual imaginative hand-pleated headings. Instructions to help you make pelmets and valances, together with three different types of blinds, are included, plus the all important sewing techniques, just in case memory fails you for one vital moment. Throughout each process I promise to pass on as many professional secrets, and shortcuts, as possible to save both your time and temper. So let me help you design individual window treatments, enjoy making them up yourself at home and cut the cost of curtaining by more than half.

Tricks of the trade are easy to spot in the text; they are set in bold type and marked with the symbol ➝ .

Acknowledgements

My grateful thanks to Camden Interiors of Clifton, Bristol, and to the helpful staff at all John Lewis stores. Also to Anna Pearson who helped me make my first curtain eighteen years ago and who has been a constant source of encouragement and inspiration.

HELEN O'LEARY
JULY 1982

1 Planning Window Treatments

Few things affect the appearance of a room more than curtains. For a start, windows should be looked at — not just through. They are, after all, the most important fixture in any room, yet frequently are the most neglected feature. Sadly, too many people take the easy way out: they hang up a pair of curtains, regardless of the shape and size of the window, and think no more about them.

Yet carefully planned curatins can create illusions of height and width. They can highlight good proportions, disguise architectural faults and, above all, set the stamp of individual style on the scene.

It is also true to say that, no matter how awkward or difficult a window's proportions, there is a way to flatter it *yourself*, easily and inexpensively — that is, at a fraction of the cost a professional curtain maker would be forced to charge. (Do forget immediately the ready-made, shop-bought curtains generally sold in packets. While the fabric may be pretty, the design is necessarily plain and unimaginative to conform with manufacturers' standards and will seldom flatter any window.)

Next let me assure you, right from the start, that there is no need to be experienced with a needle to achieve the stunning effects frequently shown in the glossy magazines. What you do need, however, is to consider your windows and their function carefully, then plan their treatment before you dash out to the shops to buy fabric. Failure to spend sufficient time at the initial stage will almost certainly produce disappointing results.

→ Here are five essential points to help set your priorities and plan successfully:

Appearance Remember that the use of texture and colour contribute to the overall design of a room.

View Do you want to see out or not? Your 'view', particularly in an inner-city area, may be a brick wall!

Privacy Bedrooms and bathrooms obviously need to be 'peeper-proof'.

Noise Fabric can not only help soak up sound from outside but also prevent the spread of sound from room to room inside. Do you or yours play musical instruments?

Light Control Too much light can damage carpets and furniture, while in dark rooms the little light available needs to be maximized.

One step further on, let's find your basic window shape.

Basic Window Shapes

Vertical Windows

How you treat this type of window depends to a large extent on the architectural style of your home.

Tall, narrow windows, often sashed, in a period house with high ceilings, present no problem. They are an asset to be emphasized. Choose formal fabrics, furnish each window with floor-to-ceiling curtains and thus accentuate their slender, graceful proportions. If you feel ambitious, make pelmets, or swags and tails too, providing they do not clash with a particularly ornate ceiling or cornice. Otherwise select a neat, interesting heading, e.g., pinch pleats, and suspend the curtains from a brass or wooden pole.

Vertical windows in a modern home with low ceilings are more complicated to dress. Your need is to minimize the height and so broaden the overall effect. Here the trick is to extend the curtain rail beyond the window frame on either side so that when the curtains are drawn back they lie flat against the wall.

Where such a scheme is impractical, consider shortening the total effect by making sill-length curtains in a patterned fabric with a horizontal theme.

Horizontal Windows

Deep picture windows or patio doors across a wall are a familiar feature in many modern homes. Clever curtain designers continue this horizontal theme with carefully chosen fabric, a neat pleated heading, and important floor-to-ceiling curtains which sweep away to one side during the day.

Where there are several small windows across a ← wall, often quite high up, use matching patterned wallpaper and fabric to minimize any unevenness, and fit the curtains to the actual height and width of the window. Use a simple gathered or pleated heading and stick a piece of fabric over the front of the track so that when the curtains are drawn back no ugly aluminium or white strips break up the patterned surface.

Bow and Bay Windows

Both these types of window enhance and enlarge a room. Sadly, the unimaginative home decorator faced with a sweeping curve simply runs curtains right across the front. Of course, it is true that this type of treatment provides maximum light during the day and saves fabric. But when drawn in the evening, the curtains cut off the bay, ruining the proportions of the room and changing its character completely.

A much better way to dress both bow or bay windows is to make a feature of them by hanging curtains from a flexible aluminium track fixed to follow the sweep of the curve. Whether you choose several small curtains or two large ones depends on the width of the frame between each window section. The small type of bow window frequently installed in the seventies will obviously only sustain one pair of curtains. However, the important thing to remember is the need for unity, so do link the effect together with a pelmet or valance.

→ **Anchor the full height (i.e. from track to floor) of the outside edges of the curtain flat against the wall to avoid unsightly gaps.**

Irregular Windows

Almost every home has at least one problem window. If you have a window shape which you feel defeats your best intentions, take heart. Here are some hints to help you meet the challenge.

Dormer Windows

Usually these are small windows with no wall space at the sides. Although they are attractive to look at, they do tend to tunnel both light and air. This means that normal window treatments will usually restrict both even more. The answer in most cases is to make roller blinds instead of curtains. Alternatively, you use light, filmy fabrics, assuming they provide the necessary feeling of privacy at night.

Arched Windows

Arched windows are architecturally expensive to install, and invariably an attractive feature of any room or hallway which it would be a pity to disregard. So here are some ideas to help you make the most of this very pretty type of window.

(a)   Frame the window: hang panels of fabric high, well above the top of the window and wide enough apart to leave the entire window exposed when the curtains are open.

(b)   Confine the curtaining to the rectangular section of the window below the arch. This is particularly suitable for a window on the stairs where large quantities of fabric are unnecessary and may present a potential hazard.

(c)   Make cafe curtains (see page 40). Use sheer fabric for the top arched part of the window and suspend separate curtains from a rod for the lower part which will draw well back.

(d)   **For a really professional, stunning look, fix two ◄— curtains permanently round the arch (use flexible track) and loop back the sides with cords or tie-backs.** See Fig. 1.

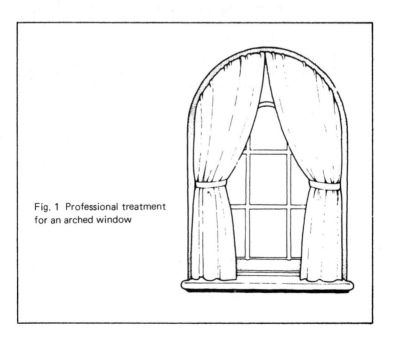

Fig. 1 Professional treatment for an arched window

Tools to Ease Your Task

Long lengths of material which need to be cut out make the work different from that of home dressmaking. Thus the most important thing you need is a really large table (a table tennis table suitably covered is ideal) or, better still, a clean carpeted floor on which to cut fabric. American curtain enthusiasts insist on a cutting board marked with square or diagonal grids to ensure sections are cut accurately. A medium-sized version can be obtained in this country in at least one of the large furnishing stores. However, I find the floor/drawn-thread method equally effective. More of this in Chapter 2.

Pins Use good-quality dressmaker's steel pins which do not rust.

→ **If you prick your finger and accidentally bleed on to the fabric, chew a length of cotton thread and dab it on to the material to remove the stain without leaving a water mark.**

Needles These must be sharp and rust-free. Keep a selection to use with various types of fabric.

Thread Match thread to your chosen fabric. Thus always use synthetic thread for nylons, polyesters and man-made fibres. Use Sylko 40 or 50 for general purposes on medium-weight fabrics.

→ *Scissors* You will need two pairs. **Scissors with extra long blades speed up the cutting process.** A smaller pair are useful for thread, etc. Always buy scissors of good quality and keep them sharp.

Metre measuring stick An inexpensive aid to accurate measurement sold in most DIY shops. No self-respecting curtain maker would be without one!

Linen tape measure The cotton sort shrinks.

Steel rule Good for measuring windows before you put up tracks or poles.

→ **A 'Quick Unpick'** Invaluable little tool for un-

picking stitches swiftly, obtainable from the haberdashery counter in department stores.

Ironing board and iron You will need both
constantly. If your board has a broad surface, so
much the better. Watch out for, and clean away, man-
made fibre deposits on the base of the iron when
using synthetic materials.

Sewing machine Because so many long seams
have to be worked when you make curtains and
drapes, a good sewing machine is almost essential.
When and if you do invest in one, remember that it is
one of the few items which can be purchased with a
view to lasting a good long time. Choose a model to
suit your individual needs. The small portable machines
are not suitable for working heavy furnishing fabrics.
And if you do not see yourself producing embroidery
or smocking by the yard, resist the temptation to buy
the elaborate automatic models. Treat whichever
type of machine you buy with care and consideration.
Always read the instruction manual thoroughly before
you begin to sew with a new or unfamiliar machine.
Better still, ask the dealer (or the owner if you are
buying secondhand) for a demonstration.

Fixtures and Fittings

The professional look of curtains comes not only
from well-chosen fabric but from many other things
you never see: the indispensable underpinnings, tracks,
tapes, rings, hooks and stiffeners, to name a few.
Let's look at some of the more important items.

Curtain Tracks and Rails

There are numerous types of track, rail and pole
currently available in a wide variety of materials,
e.g., brass, plastic and aluminium. Spend a little time

exploring the full range. Compare the different makes on the market and analyse their various functions before you spend any money. When you do make a decision, remember that the type of track you choose must depend on the following points:

(a) Your proposed window treatment. Keep a rough sketch of your plan in your pocket for easy reference.

(b) The style of heading you wish to use. For example, if your design includes a pelmet, both the heading and track will be out of sight and can therefore be of the simplest kind. Sophisticated pinch pleats, on the other hand, look best suspended from a smart, transverse cord-operated rod.

(c) The weight of your chosen fabric. Inexpensive extruded-plastic track is fine for filmy sheers or light cotton fabrics but quite unable to support heavy velvet, brocade or interlined curtains. Strong aluminium track or sturdy wooden poles are the best answer for long, heavy curtains.

Whichever type of track or pole you choose, however, do make sure you buy all the necessary attachments and fittings at the same time. It can be very frustrating trailing from shop to shop, searching for out-of-stock or obsolete accessories.

Hooks

Curtain hooks are attached to the curtain heading and then inserted through runners or gliders on the curtain track. Again, there are plenty of designs from which to choose. Small plastic or metal hooks with a double bend plus a small extra bend are mostly used with simple drawing tapes. Long-pronged hooks slot into specially designed pleating tape both to stiffen the heading and form the pleats. (Make sure you buy hooks to match your chosen tape — there are several slightly different styles.) Simple brass hooks are used mostly for hand-pleated headings — although some people use a type of brass hook which requires no stitching on hand-gathered headings thus saving time.

Curtain Tapes

All well-made curtains have some form of heading tape to provide a firm base for the hooks. Heading tapes basically fall into two categories: the many different types of drawing tapes which, when applied to the curtain, are then drawn up to produce gathers, pleats or a smocking effect; or the simple, strong heading tape normally used with hand-pleated headings.

Pull-cords

Constant handling of curtains soils and spoils the fabric. Pull-cords are a practical way to deal with curtains where a cording set is not an integral part of the curtain track.

Weights

Small lead weights can be bought strung on tapes or encased in cord ready to insert into hems to make curtains hang straight and smooth. **Weights also** ⟵ **provide ballast for corners** (see Fig. 3 on page 28).

Fabric Choice and Care

Choosing your fabric for curtains should be fun. But buy in haste and you will certainly regret at leisure. So take time to visit several different types of fabric supplier before you make your final selection. The furnishing fabric hall in a large department store is a good place to make a start; there you can see a really wide selection of materials in stock. Then check out any local discount houses, which frequently offer the keenest prices, particularly for linings. Finally, remember the small interior design shops; these are often a source for the more unusual designs and fabrics, sometimes at surprisingly modest prices.

Here are a few tips to help you enjoy the search and choose wisely:

(a) Consider suitability: for the room, function and wearability. In America furnishing fabrics carry labels concerning the care, durability, and stain and soil resistance of the material. Here we are not so lucky, but some curtainings have a fadeproof guarantee. Watch out for this if you are proposing to sew unlined curtains.

(b) Buy only curtain fabric. Material marked as suitable for upholstery often has a higher cotton content which will induce creasing.

(c) Take care when choosing patterned fabrics. Large pattern repeats can involve you in a considerable amount of extra expenditure. Smaller patterns require less fabric and are thus more economical.

→ (d) **Before reaching a final conclusion, ask to see fabric draped. Patterns and texture look very different lying flat on a counter.**

(e) Even if you know sewing curtains will take you for ever, do buy sufficient material to complete the task. Colour and patterns are often difficult to match exactly at a later date.

(f) Take a sketch of your proposed window treatment to the shop, together with the exact measurements. Discuss your plans with the salesman/woman and let them check your fabric requirements. They are usually very experienced at estimating materials and eager to help you achieve good results.

When it comes to choosing fabrics for blinds, bear in mind the following points:

Roman blinds need to be made from sturdy fabric, reinforced by lining, in order to have sufficient body to fold evenly and hang plumb.

Festoon blinds should be made with lightweight fabric which ruches gracefully and falls in puffy folds.

18

Roller blinds are best made from specially stiffened materials often sold in the haberdashery departments of large stores.

Linings

Apart from those for kitchen or bathroom, all curtains look best lined. A good lining not only protects the main fabric from dirt, dust and sunlight but also gives a uniform look to the outside of your home. In addition, some linings provide an extra source of insulation, e.g., the metallic variety, popular since the sixties, or the newer, less expensive thermal lining — a plain white bonded cotton fabric.

However, cotton sateen is the fabric most generally used to line curtains. It can be bought in a wide range of colours and in many different qualities. Colour, of course, depends upon your personal preference but on no account attempt to economize on quality. Loosely woven, cheaper varieties of sateen, often imported, can cause your carefully sewn curtains to drop after only a few weeks; will almost certainly shrink with cleaning; and have even been known to rot after relatively little wear.

Sateen lining is sold in 122 cm widths, but do ← **check at the time of purchase because some can be as wide as 183 cm, while some 'bargains' are very narrow indeed which is often why they are being sold cheaply.**

Interlining

This is a soft, loosely woven fabric used to give body to curtains and provide insulation. (Silk or cotton curtains made up with interlining look sumptuous.) The materials used are bump or domette. Bump is a thick, fluffy fabric made from cotton waste usually 122 cm wide. Domette, although similar, is not quite so thick and fluffy. Neither fabric is washable, thus *all interlined curtains must be dry-cleaned only*.

The Question of Care

Being good to your curtains can extend their life span. Fabrics vary in the care they need, but they all need your help. Monthly brushing by hand or vacuum cleaning will remove surface dust, but more radical cleaning is needed at least once a year. However, because of their size or construction, many curtains are impossible to launder at home, so choose the best dry-cleaner in the district. On the other hand, even if the curtains are washable, remember that stiffeners and trims may not take to water as happily as the curtain fabric.

The following fabrics must be dry-cleaned: all velvets, velours, chenilles, tapestries and brocades, together with all fabrics containing wool or silk, plus all pelmets, curtains or valences into which buckram has been inserted.

Fabrics which may be washed with care are: colour-fast cottons, linens, polyester mixtures, nets and sheers made from man-made fibres. In all cases check the washing instructions — some fabrics must not be put in the tumble-drier or ironed.

Glassfibre fabrics, although not much in use now, should be mentioned because they must be washed by hand and drip-dried. Iron or dry-clean them at your peril.

→ **Window condensation may cause staining no cleaner can remove. Be sure to suspend curtains so that your expensive fabric does not touch the glass.**

2 Lined, Unlined and Interlined Curtains and Tie-backs

'When can we get down to actually sewing the curtains?' You may well ask! The short answer is: 'Not quite yet.' There are still a couple of points to be sorted out before you dash to the shops and buy fabric, never mind start to stitch! The points to consider are:

(a) Your choice of heading.
(b) The overall size of the curtains.

Undoubtedly your budget will be the most important single factor to influence any decision on both. For example, short sill-length curtains require less fabric and are thus more economical than their glamorous floor-length counterparts. On the other hand, full-length elegance need not cost a fortune if you suspend the curtains from rods or tracks hidden by a pelmet or valance, since the required fabric width for this type of treatment is only one and a half times the length of the track.

However, if you prefer the prestigious look of an elaborate, deep-pleated heading, be prepared to pay for your pleasure; some headings of this type require a fabric width of two and a half or even three times the length of the track.

Whatever style of curtain you choose, never skimp on fullness. Lots of cheap cotton fabric looks much better than too little expensive velvet.

Measuring Up

Once your plans are finalized, the next step is to measure accurately the actual area the curtain is to cover. **For successful curtains you must start with the correct measurements. That is why professional curtain makers always place the pole or track in position** *before* **they measure for fabric. So buy and fix your** track first; and then measure with a steel rule or wooden metre stick. Here's how (see Fig. 2):

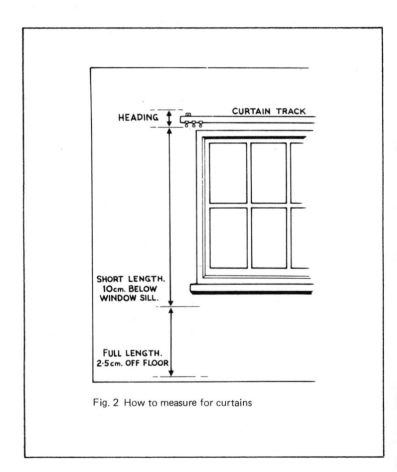

Fig. 2 How to measure for curtains

Length

Measure the drop from the base of the glider or ring on the track to the required length. Allow for an extra 10 cm below the sill for short curtains and make full-length curtains fall within 2 to 2.3 cm of the floor or carpet. **Make velvet or other heavy curtains** ← **very slightly shorter to allow for them to drop slightly when hung.**

Measure from the base of the glider or ring on the track upwards for the required heading. Allow approximately 2.5 cm for a simple gathering tape and between 5 and 15 cm for the more elaborate varieties.

Allow 7.5 cm for turning at the top of the curtain.
Allow 15 cm for the lower hem.

With the above measurements, make use of the standard curtain makers' formula:

Length or drop = hook drop + heading + turning + hem.

Width

Begin by measuring the width of the *track* not the ← **window.** Then multiply the figure by that of your chosen heading (e.g. 1½ for a simple gathered heading), add 30 cm for side turnings plus overlap, and this gives you the total width of fabric required. Divide this figure by 2 if you are making a pair of curtains.

The curtain makers' standard equation to remember is:

Track length x 1½ (simple gathered heading)
+ 30 cm ÷ 2 = the width of each curtain.

If you plan a return to the wall at the outer edge of the curtains, add that depth to the length of the curtain track.

Estimating the Total Amount of Fabric Required

To find out the total length of fabric you need,

multiply the required length by the number of widths needed to cover the window. In order to do this easy sum, you need to know how many widths of fabric are needed in *each* curtain. Here's an example to help you calculate correctly:

To make one curtain measuring 193 cm wide, you need to join together one and a half widths of fabric 122 cm wide. Thus, to make curtains measuring 193 cm each, you need three widths of fabric 122 cm wide.

Where it is necessary to join together an odd number of widths of fabric (three is the usual number of widths for a pair of curtains), always place complete panels at the centre of the curtains with the two half-width sections down each outer edge.

If your chosen fabric is patterned, allow one pattern repeat per width of curtain required.

Because of their diverse countries of origin, curtain fabrics are sold in varying widths ranging from 122 to 137 cm. To be safe and thus sure, always assume for the purposes of your calculations that all fabrics are 122 cm wide.

Cutting Out

It is absolutely essential that curtain lengths are cut straight across the fabric. Even a small mistake at this stage can make your curtains hang unevenly. **A tip worth knowing is that professional curtain makers wherever possible draw a couple of threads across the width of the fabric to use as a cutting guide.** So do follow their example when you use straight-woven fabrics.

Linens, chintz and cotton-printed fabrics present more of a problem: the grain of the fabric is frequently unstable due to the looseness of the weave; while the pattern is sometimes stretched out of line during the printing process. The way to overcome these diffi-

24

culties is to place a metre stick at right angles to the selvedge of the fabric and chalk on a cutting line. Or you could make up a 'cutting board', a piece of equipment much in favour in America. Alternatively, try this excellent tip I had from an accomplished yet thrifty curtain maker: **place your fabric on a rectangular table** ← **with the selvedge running down the length of the long side. Then use the end of the table to square up the fabric and mark in a cutting line.**

Besides being straight, panels of patterned fabric must match. Mentally rearranging an unmatched pattern on a pair of curtains can be very irritating. Some fabrics do match equally at the selvedge; others, in fact the majority of patterned fabrics, do not, and these have what the trade terms 'a pattern drop'. When you buy this type of material, remember to allow extra metreage to cover the drop. Assistants in large furnishing-fabric stores are usually very helpful and knowledgeable about pattern repeats and drops. **However, a quick way to work out the extra** ← **fabric requirement yourself is to allow for one pattern repeat on each length of curtain you cut out. Plan to finish at the same position of the pattern on each panel.**

Finally, here are a few hints to help you cut out with confidence:

(a) Before you take up the scissors:

(i) Measure and mark, with pins or chalk, the position of your cutting line.

(ii) Re-check that you have allowed sufficient fabric for turnings and pattern repeats or drops.

(b) **Mark the *top* of each panel of fabric as you cut** ← **it from the roll. This is essential when you use velours or velvets, where the pile should run *down* the curtains.**

(c) Cut away the selvedge to prevent puckering. Some people prefer merely to clip the selvedge at 5-cm intervals, but I have always found it best to remove them completely.

(d)   Remember to cut away and discard any wastage immediately on a patterned fabric to avoid confusion at a later stage.

How to Make Up Curtains

Any professional curtain maker, when asked for advice, will almost certainly reply, 'Make your curtains from the bottom up.' To the novice, such a statement seems at first impossible. Friends given the above tip nearly always go on to ask, 'How can I get the hems exactly right without hanging the curtains first?' Let me assure you, and them yet again, that if you do hang your curtains before completing the bottom hems, the chances are that you will never get those hems straight!

The secret of success lies in taking exact measurements in the first place, plus constantly checking those measurements every 10 cm as you apply the heading tape. Then, in the unlikely event of the curtains needing a slight adjustment at the hanging stage, this can be quickly made — either by changing the position of the hooks (on a hand-pleated heading) or re-applying the heading tape. With a 'Quick Unpick', commercial tape can be ripped off in a couple of seconds, then machined back into place at the adjusted level, and the whole operation completed in less than half an hour. Correcting the bottom hem is much more time-consuming as it includes re-mitring the corners and adjusting the lining and interlining, and unpicking a carefully hand-worked hem can be heartbreaking. Worse, the difficulty of laying the completed curtain out flat once the heading pleats have been made means the end result is unlikely to prove satisfactory. So please, when making up your curtains, start at the bottom and finish at the top.

The next step is to learn the basic method for making curtains and, since this is much the same whether or not the curtains are to be lined, it is advisable to master the technique for making unlined curtains first, before you attempt the lined or inter-lined variety.

The main differences in the construction of lined and unlined curtains are that in the former widths need only a plain open seam and simple turned-in hems down each side, while in the latter widths must be joined by a machine run and seam and have *double* hems down each long side and across the bottom edge.

Method for Making Unlined Curtains

(a) Cut out the curtains carefully. Remove the selvedges. If using more than one width of fabric in each curtain, seam the panels together. Make sure the pattern matches at the seam line. Use a machine and fell seam (see Chapter 8) for both strength and appearance.

If you prefer to retain the selvedges, clip them every ⟵ 5 cm along the length of the curtain and apply a flat seam. Press the seam open.

(b) Place the completed panels right side down on a table or on the floor and, working on the wrong side of the fabric, pin a 3-cm double hem down each side of the curtain. Slipstitch the hems into place.

(c) Turn up, pin and tack a double hem 7.5 cm deep at the bottom edge of the curtain. Mitre the corners (see Chapter 8 for details) and enclose the weights if you are using them (see Fig. 3).

(d) Turn the top of the curtain down 7.5 cm to the wrong side of the fabric.

(e) Apply the chosen heading tape (see Chapter 3) with machine stitching. Remove the tacking. Apply hooks or split rings. Draw the curtain up to the required width.

(f) **Hang the curtains and set the folds, a favourite ⟵ professional dodge to ensure crisp pleats. Open the**

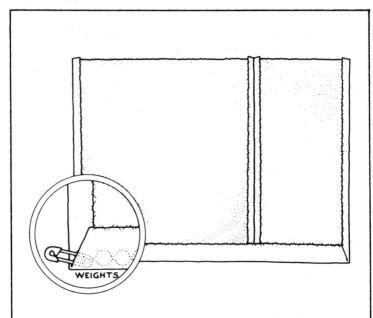

Fig. 3 Unlined curtain made from one and a half widths of fabric with weights at the corner to add balast

curtain fully and from the top form neat folds by finger-pressing down each pleat or fold for 30 cm or so. Tie loosely with a scrap of material. For full-length curtains repeat the process, making two or three ties down the length of the curtain. Leave the ties in position for two to three days for the fabric to develop a 'memory'.

Method for Making Lined Curtains

There are three ways to make up lined curtains: the bag method; with detachable loose linings; and with locked-in linings.

The Bag Method

Many busy people favour this way of making lined curtains principally because the entire operation can be performed with a minimum of fuss on a simple sewing machine. No particular skill is required and there are no tricks of the trade to divulge. But because no book on curtains would be complete without mentioning the method, here, for all non-sewing, busy people, is a brief explanation of what to do.

(a) Measure the track and drop of your window and calculate the amount of fabric required, bearing in mind your chosen heading. See Chapter 3 under 'Curtain Headings Made With Commercial Tapes'.

(b) Cut out the main fabric and seam together any necessary widths.

(c) Cut out the lining 2.5 cm smaller than the main fabric all round. If you fail to do this, the lining will curl round to the front of the curtain no matter how much it is pressed.

(d) Pin the right side of the lining to the right side of the main fabric. Machine stitch three of the four sides together in exactly the same way as you would if you were to make a shoe bag. Turn the curtain right side out. Tuck in the top.

(e) Apply the heading tape and insert the hooks into the woven pockets on the tape.

Detachable Loose Linings

At first glance, detachable loose linings seem the answer to a prayer. They are quick and easy to make, and they can be removed for cleaning or changed from one set of curtains to another in a matter of moments. Their practicality depends on the fact that they are made with their own special lining tape and are therefore quite separate from the main curtains. They simply share the same hooks from which the curtain is suspended from the track.

However, in spite of their many advantages, curtains with detachable linings somehow miss the smooth professional look gained from locked-in linings. To overcome this, some curtain makers slipstitch or tack the linings to the curtain down each long side to unite the two fabrics and prevent the tendency for the lining to show at the outer edges. This course of action seems to me to defeat the object of the exercise — namely that the linings should be detachable!

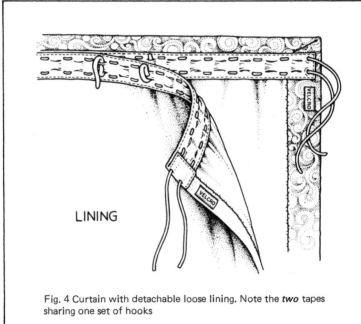

Fig. 4 Curtain with detachable loose lining. Note the *two* tapes sharing one set of hooks

Professional curtain makers prefer to stick strips of touch-and-close fastening (Velcro is the best-known) to both lining and main fabric at intervals down the long sides and thus avoid any chance of the lining and curtain parting company, while at the same time retaining the practical aspect of detachable linings.

The method to follow when making detachable linings is as follows:

(a) Make up the curtains in the main fabric in the usual way (page 29).

(b) Cut out the linings to the same dimensions, but make the length 2.5 cm shorter than that of the main fabric, measuring from the heading tape to the base of the hem.

(c) Apply the lining tape in the following way:
>   (i) Cut the lining heading tape to the required width plus 7.5 cm for turnings.
>
>   (ii) Pull the cords free from each end of the tape for 4 cm.
>
>   (iii) At one end knot the cords together, and leave the other end free.
>
>   (iv) Fold the knotted cord under the tape and stitch into position.
>
>   (v) Lay the tape right side up on a table.
>
>   (vi) Feed the lining right side up between the two layers of the tape and pin and tack into position, extending the tape 3.5 cm at either end of the lining fabric.
>
>   (vii) Tuck surplus tape under at each end to lie level with the lining tape.
>
>   (viii) Machine along the lower edge of the tape through all three thicknesses, i.e. through tape/lining/tape.

(d) Pull up the cord ends to make the lining 5 cm narrower than your curtain. Knot off the cords.

(e) Slip the hooks first into the slits in the lining tape, then into the pockets of the curtain heading tape, and turn into their final position.

Your curtains are now ready to hang.

Locked-in Linings

The best way to approach making this type of lined curtains, particularly if you are a complete novice, is to break the job down into three stages. The following three short sets of instructions should help you feel confident to tackle the task and at the same time make the work seem easy.

Main Fabric

(a)   Measure and cut out the material carefully. Remember to match up any pattern repeats. Remove selvedge.

(b)   Plain seam (see Chapter 8) the widths or half-widths together to form complete curtain panels. Press open the seams.

(c)   Turn the fabric in 6 cm down each of the long sides, and make a 7.5-cm double hem across the bottom edge. Pin, tack and then use a large hem stitch for all three sides.

→ (d)   Mitre the corners. **To make a perfect mitre, both hems should be equal, but it is not really important here. Some curtain makers use only a 6-cm hem across the bottom but the extra depth helps the curtain to hang more gracefully.**

Lining

(a)   Cut out the lining to the same measurements as the main fabric. Remove all selvedges.

(b)   Plain seam the widths or half-widths together to form complete panels. Press open the seams.

To Apply the Lining

(a)   Spread the main fabric out on a flat surface, *wrong* side uppermost. Now here's a tip to keep your
→ stitches, and incidentally the fabric, straight: **measure and draw vertical lines, 30 cm apart, down the wrong**

side of the fabric. Use tailor's chalk for this.

(b) Place the lining over the curtain fabric, *wrong* side down (i.e., with the two wrong sides together). Position the lining approximately 2 cm from the top of the curtain.

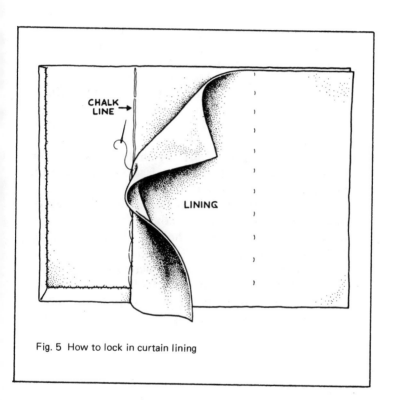

Fig. 5 How to lock in curtain lining

(c) Carefully fold back the lining from the left to the first chalk guide line on the right side. Lockstitch the lining into position (see Chapter 8). Begin your stitches 15 cm from the top of the curtain and make them 10 cm apart. Be careful not to pull the thread too tightly or the main fabric may pucker. Pick up only one thread of the main fabric at each stitch. Once the line is completed, bring the lining forward to the next and repeat the locking process. Continue across the curtain as necessary.

Always use thread for locking which matches the *main fabric*, not the lining.

(d) Once the lines of locking are completed, trim away any excess lining fabric extending beyond the curtain edge. (To recap, this means that the lining should lie flush with the main fabric down both the long sides and across the bottom edge.)

(e) Fold in the lining 2.5 cm and pin in position down both long sides and across the bottom edge. Make sure the corner of the lining meets the mitre on the main fabric.

→ **(f) Now, to hold the fabrics securely in position for further stitching, make a line of tacking 5 cm from the top right across the curtain.**

(g) Slipstitch the lining to the main fabric down both the long sides and across the bottom edge. Begin the stitching 15 cm from the top of the curtain to allow for the heading.

(h) Remove the line of tacking across the top of the curtain. Turn in both the main fabric and the lining. Press. Add the stiffening, if you propose to make a hand-pleated heading, or apply your chosen commercial heading tape. Add the hooks and hang the curtain.

Interlining

Interlining gives curtains extra body and the luxury look. It also provides a certain amount of insulation. However, interlining adds considerably to the overall cost of curtaining. To help you determine whether the increased cost is justified, consider your planned window treatment, the weight of your chosen fabric and whether or not your windows are double-glazed.

Remember also that most interior designers working to a small budget prefer to recommend their client to install all curtains made from generous amounts of inexpensive fabric, e.g., cotton, lined and interlined, rather than use a more expensive fabric with a simple lining.

You need **exactly the same amount of interlining** ← **fabric as for the** *finished flat* **curtain.**

This is what you do:

(a) Cut out the main fabric and lining for the curtain. Join together widths where necessary.

(b) Cut the interlining to the exact size of the final finished flat curtain. **Join together widths where** ← **necessary by overlapping the raw edge of the wrong side of one length with the edge of the right side of another length. Join with two rows of machine stitch-**

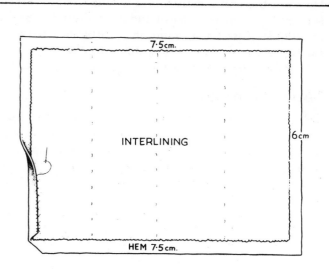

Fig. 6 Interlining cut to the finished flat curtain size, locked into the main fabric and applied to the main fabric with catchstitch

ing. Bump and domette stretch, hence the double row of stitching to provide extra strength.

(c) Spread out the main fabric on a table or floor, wrong side uppermost. Position the interlining over the wrong side of the curtain 7.5 cm from the top, leaving 6 cm borders down both sides of the main fabric.

(d) Fold back the interlining from the left to within 12 cm from the right and lockstitch into position. You need to stitch approximately three rows of locking every 120 cm. Detailed instructions for locked-in linings are provided on page 32.

(e) Turn the edges of the main fabric down the long sides and across the hem over on to the interlining. Herringbone/catchstitch into position and mitre the corners.

(f) Place the lining over the interlining, fold in the usual 2.5 cm at the sides and along the bottom edge. Match mitres and slipstitch into position.

(g) Fold down the top of the main fabric over the interlining. Insert any additional stiffening. Turn in the top of the lining and slipstitch into place.

(h) Apply the chosen heading.

Shower Curtains

Shower curtains can be made in two ways. The first and by far the more effective is to make up an unlined curtain to match the window curtains and add a detachable showerproof lining. (See page 27 for how to make unlined curtains and page 29 for details of detachable linings.)

Simple plastic fabric shower curtains, on the other hand, require a minimum of stitching, are relatively inexpensive and can be made up in under an hour.

Plastic Fabric Shower Curtains

When estimating the amount of fabric required,

remember that shower curtains can be up to one and a half times the width of the rail but fullness is not particularly necessary. Allow 5 cm of extra material for each side hem, 5 cm for the bottom hem and 10 cm for the heading. Do not forget to calculate for any pattern repeats if necessary.

From your local soft-furnishing specialist buy some dual-purpose shower-curtain hooks which act both as hooks and runners. Next, beg, borrow or buy a special eyelet hole punch. Use nylon or other synthetic thread for sewing and **adhesive tape or paper clips** ← **instead of pins for tacking.**

When you machine stitch a plastic fabric, always use a long, loose stitch to avoid any excess tension. **A tiny drop of sewing machine lubricant applied to** ← **the tip of the needle will make stitching easier.**

The method to follow is:

(a) Join together any necessary widths of material. Use a French seam (see Chapter 8) to keep the curtain water-tight.

(b) Turn in and machine stitch double hems 2.5 cm deep down each long side and the bottom edge of the curtain.

(c) Turn over a 5 cm double hem at the top, but do not stitch down. Instead use the hole punch to make metal-trimmed eyelet holes 5 cm apart along the top of the curtain.

(d) Insert the dual-purpose hooks into the eyelet holes and hang the curtain from the shower rail.

If you are unable to obtain an eyelet hole punch, stitch a nylon heading tape along the top of the curtain. It will work perfectly well, although the extra stitching must eventually weaken the plastic fabric.

Tie-backs

Tie-backs have been used, in one form or another, at

least in England, since the sixteenth century when fairly heavy curtains for windows or beds were caught back with silk or golden cord tassels in natural-looking folds to let in light. Today they are back in fashion to perform much the same function, although occasionally they are used as a purely decorative feature in conjunction with dress curtains.

Many types of commercially made cords, tassels and gilded metal tie-backs are available from good furnishing stores. Yet simple unshaped or shaped tie-backs, made from fabric which matches that of the curtains, are far less costly, much more charming and easily made at home — another way to add that important individual touch to your window treatment.

To Make an Unshaped Tie-back

(a)   To calculate the length of the tie-back, measure round the curtain, take in as much fullness as necessary, and add an extra 2 cm. The extra 2 cm is to provide sufficient fabric for the hooks. The finished depth of

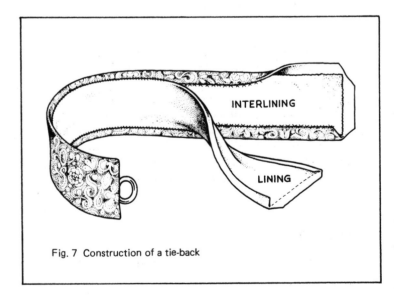

Fig. 7 Construction of a tie-back

a tie-back is usually about 10 cm, but this can be varied to suit the proportions of the window. These two measurements now make up the final size of your completed tie-back.

(b) Cut a strip of interlining to the exact size of your completed tie-back.

(c) Cut out the main fabric and lining. Use the above measurements plus 1.5 cm extra all round.

(d) Shape the ends of the tie-back fabric into points or curves.

(e) Position and tack the interlining to the wrong side of the main fabric. Turn the main fabric over the interlining 1.5 cm all round. Press and catchstitch/herringbone into position.

(f) Place the lining over the interlining, right side up. Turn the edges of the lining in so that they finish 0.5 cm in from edge of the tie-back. Pin, press and slipstitch into position. Attach rings or hooks at each end and screw a hook into the wall or window reveal.

For a crisp, neat finish when you use a lightweight ←
or sheer fabric, attach a strip of buckram, cut to the same size, to the interlining to provide extra stiffening.

To Make a Shaped Tie-back

Traditional crescent-shaped tie-backs can look particularly attractive. Their gentle, upward curves hold the curtain fullness in check, while the lower edges can be scalloped or decorated with braid or piping.

Again, this type of tie-back is not difficult to make. The trick is to experiment first with a paper pattern. First draw one half of your chosen shape on a folded sheet of paper. Make the centre of the tie-back at the fold of the paper to ensure symmetry. Cut out the paper pattern and try it round the curtain for size and shape. If you are not quite satisfied, start again. Remember that it is important to make all tie-backs sufficiently loose to allow the curtains to appear to their full advantage.

Once a satisfactory design has been produced, the procedure is as follows:

→ (a) **Place the folded pattern on double fabric and cut out both sides of the tie-back at one time.** Allow 1.5 cm for turnings all round.

(b) Cut out the lining in exactly the same way. Again, allow 1.5 cm for turnings.

(c) Cut out the interlining and any stiffener to the same size as the finished tie-back. Do not allow for turnings.

(d) Finish in the same way as for unshaped tie-backs, described above.

Cafe Curtains

The charm of cafe curtains lies in their versatility. They provide a casual, relaxed look; they can be made in multiple tiers of varying lengths, any of which can be opened or closed independently; and they lend themselves to almost any type of heading that suits your mood and room.

Basic cafe curtains usually comprise two small pairs of curtains, one each for the lower and upper parts of the window. Thus two tracks or poles are needed, one at the top of the window and one half-way up. Scalloped headings are frequently chosen for both curtains.

Single-tier cafe curtains are simply half-length curtains, often with a scalloped heading, used to screen an ugly view or provide privacy for the occupants of a room. For example, imaginative American designers may use sheer cafe curtains teamed with frothy dress curtains in bedrooms and bathrooms, instead of the more traditional single nets commonly seen in Britain. One glossy magazine recently even showed an impressive three-tier arrangement of white

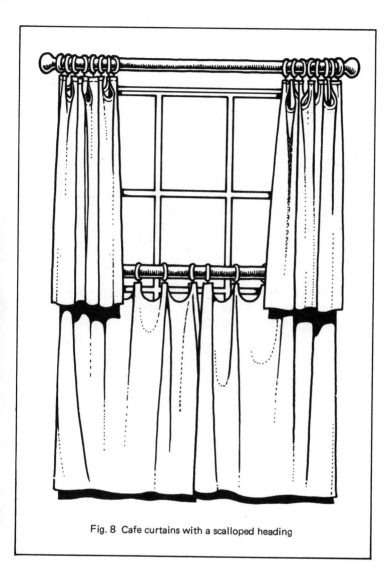

Fig. 8 Cafe curtains with a scalloped heading

nets on scarlet poles, trimmed with a scarlet bobble fringe.

Cafe curtains are constructed in the same way as lined or unlined curtains, except on occasions where a scalloped heading is used. **Remember to fix both poles or tracks before you measure for fabric.** Then let your imagination and natural flair have a chance to shine.

The length of cafe curtains naturally varies according to style. When estimating fabric requirements remember that for single-tier curtains — or for the lower panel of two-tier curtains — you should measure from the lower edge of the track to the lower edge of the window sill and add 15 cm for the hem, plus the depth of the chosen heading.

For the top panels of two-tier curtains, measure from the lower edge of the top track to the lower edge of the lower track and add 15 cm for the hem, plus an allowance for your chosen heading.

Fabric width will depend on your chosen heading; scalloped headings need only one to one and a half times the length of the track.

3 Curtain Headings

All curtains are made with some sort of heading. The question is whether you wish to stitch yours by hand or use commercial tape. Both have their own particular advantages.

Commercial tapes are available in a wide variety of styles and colours and are undoubtedly the quickest and easiest way to head curtains. There are no pleats to plot and pin into place, and they are suitable for easy-care laundering or dry-cleaning as the strings can simply be loosened and hooks removed. The whole process can be completed in less than an afternoon. Even so, all styles still have to be tacked into position, a few hooks inserted and the curtain tried out at the window to check the positioning of the tape before the final machining.

Individually designed hand-made headings certainly give a more professional finish to curtains, but the work is time-consuming. Perhaps that is why many of the less exclusive curtain makers now use commercial tapes to some extent. However, the task of sewing headings yourself can be enormously satisfying, and provide curtains with an extra touch of elegance at a fraction of the cost of professional work, or even of the commercial deep-pleater, hooks and tapes.

The choice is yours.

Headings Made With Commercial Tapes

Commercial heading tapes are available in two basic styles: drawing tape, which is used for simple gathered headings, pencil pleats and some types of pinch pleats; and slotted tape, used with long-pronged hooks to

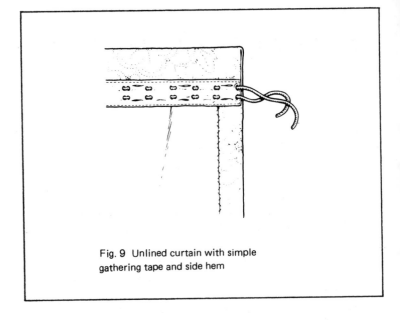

Fig. 9 Unlined curtain with simple gathering tape and side hem

produce a variety of single, double or triple pinch pleats.

All types of drawing tape, whatever the make or width, are applied in precisely the same way. So keep the following set of simple rules at your elbow and ensure success every time.

How to Apply Drawing Tape

(a) Measure the width of the curtain, and cut the tape to this width, adding 3 cm for turnings.

(b) Measure the curtains from the bottom up to ensure correct placing of the tape. (See individual instructions for positioning specific tapes at the top of the curtain.)

(c) Pin the tape across the curtain. **Check your measurements from the bottom up, every 10 to 12 cm, for a really accurate result.** A crooked tape means curtains of uneven length.

44

(d) Tack the tape to the curtain, slip in a hook or two and check against your window.

(e) Ease the cords from the last 1.5 cm of tape at each end. Tie one pair of ends in a reef knot. Tuck in the ends. Leave the other pair of cords free.

(f) Machine stitch the tape into place, carefully avoiding the two loose ends of cord. **Stitch along the** ← **top edge of the tape first. Remove from the machine and stitch the bottom edge in the same direction. This prevents puckering.**

(g) Draw the free part of the cords up to make the curtain the required width. Distribute the fullness, then tie the cords firmly, but do not cut them off. Instead wind them round a 'cord tidy' (obtainable in packs of four for a few pence) and tuck the tidy into the last pocket of the tape.

Drawing up bulky curtains can be heavy work and ← **quite hard on the hands. A tip to help is: knot one set of cords at one end and loop them round a door handle; then, holding the other pair of cords, work the curtain up towards the door.**

Simple Gathered Heading

This type of heading is suitable for use under a pelmet or valance, or where only a small frill is required. Use a standard cotton or man-made mixture tape 2.5 cm wide, with woven pockets at intervals to accommodate hooks or split rings. The fabric width required is at least one and a half times the length of the track.

To apply the tape, position it across the width of the curtain, 2 cm below the point where a pelmet or valance will be used or to 3—5 cm from the top edge for curtains with a frill. **Since this type of tape is not** ← **stiffened, for a neat crisp frill, stiffen the top 5 cm of the curtain with iron-on dress interfacing or buckram** — see the instructions under 'Hand-pleated Headings', page 50.

Pencil-pleated Heading

All commercial tapes for this type of heading are drawing tapes, that is to say they work on exactly the same principle as the simple gathered tapes. However, they are available in a variety of widths from approximately 6.5 to 15 cm and in two basic styles: those which require long-pronged hooks to help the heading to stand straight; and those stiffened with woven nylon thread which require no extra support or stiffening. Ordinary brass or plastic curtain hooks or split rings may be used with the second type of tape.

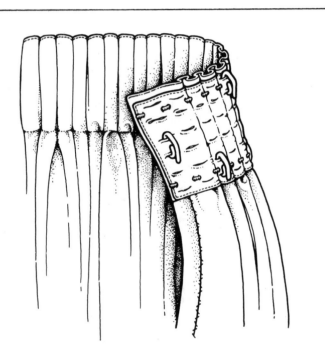

Fig. 10 Pencil-pleated heading. This tape has three rows of slots which allow the hook position to be varied according to the heading height or curtain drop required

It is also possible to buy pencil-pleating tapes with ← three alternative suspension points, useful for fabrics you fear may shrink.

To apply the tape, position it with the top approximately 2 cm below the top edge of the curtain and proceed as for drawing tape on page 44.

If you are using the type of tape which requires long-pronged hooks (see Fig. 11), check the manufacturer's instructions to make sure you apply the tape with the pockets for the hooks in the correct position — i.e., with the pockets accessible.

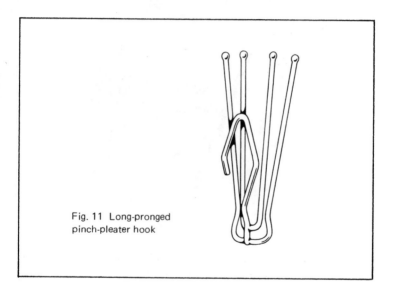

Fig. 11 Long-pronged pinch-pleater hook

Pinch-pleated Heading

Again, tapes for this type of heading fall into two categories: drawing tapes which form three pleats, followed by a flat section all along the top of the curtain when the strings are pulled up; and slotted tapes with woven pockets, into which pleater hooks are inserted at regular intervals. The advantage of using the latter variety is that you can vary the number of pleats to suit your curtain plan. Make single, double, or triple pleats — the choice is yours.

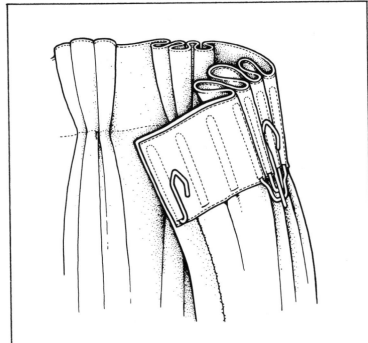

Fig. 12 Pinch pleats made from slotted tape and pronged hooks. Note how a single long-pronged hook is used for the outer edge of the curtain

The fabric width required when using this type of heading will to some extent depend on your design. Drawing tape and slotted triple pleats require two and a half times the length of the track; single slotted pleats only one and three-quarter times the length of the track.

To apply drawing tape, proceed in exactly the same way as for simple gathered tape but be sure to arrange the pleats symmetrically. **If the window frame ←— has a return at the outer edge, do not gather the curtain at this point. Instead, arrange the tape so that there is a single hook at the outer edge and allow the first pleat to fall at the corner of the return.**

To apply slotted tape, adopt the following procedure. Cut the tape to the width of the curtain, plus 3 cm for turnings. Pin the top of the tape into position 2 cm from the top of the curtain. Tuck in both ends. Carefully machine stitch all round the tape. Consider the overlap and return of your window treatment and then insert deep-pleater hooks, which have four prongs, into the woven pockets on the tape. To produce single pleats, push each of the two centre prongs into two separate pockets; for double pleats use three prongs; and for triple pleats push all four prongs into four pockets. Remember that the best way to organize this type of pleating is to arrange a single pleat at each end and then space the remaining hooks evenly along the curtain.

For an especially sophisticated look, pinch the ←— triple pleats together with a small stitch at the base of each group and add a self-covered button.

Smocked Heading

Another attractive heading which can be achieved with commercial tape is the smocked heading, which is made with a special variety of drawing tape. **Popular ←— with interior decorators, this requires only a modest amount of fabric – just twice the width of the track in each curtain, and if you're pushed for funds it can be made up with only 80 per cent fullness.** It is an exceptionally pretty heading which gives a professional finish to both main curtains and nets. Apply the tape using the instructions on page 44.

Box-pleated Heading

Produced with another style of commercial drawing tape, the box-pleated heading is useful for pelmets and valances as well as curtains. Fabric requirement is two and a half times the length of the track or area to be covered. Apply the tape in exactly the same way as any other drawing tape, but watch out for any special instructions from the manufacturers.

Hand-pleated Headings

Most beginners are afraid to tackle hand-pleated headings for curtains, yet the techniques required are not particularly arduous to learn; although finding

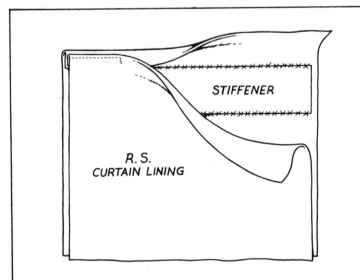

Fig. 13 Buckram or stiffener applied to the wrong side of the main fabric

sufficient time to cope with the sewing might be another matter! However, once you see your first finished hand-headed curtains hanging, you will be so pleased with their appearance that you will probably never want to use commercial tapes again; at least, not for any special window treatments.

The secret for all types of hand-pleated heading lies ← in stiffening the top 10 to 12 cm of the curtain first (see Fig. 13). Do this with buckram or any other type of heavyweight dressmaking stiffening, either the iron-on variety or the sort that requires sewing into the fabric. Both are equally satisfactory.

To stiffen any type of heading, cut the buckram, ← 10 cm wide, to the width of the finished flat curtain. Tack the stiffening to the wrong side of the main fabric approximately 7.5 cm below the top of the curtain. Make sure that you get it straight. Iron or catchstitch the stiffener into final position. Cover with the lining and continue to complete the curtain in the usual way. Lastly, stitch in your chosen style of pleats.

Pencil Pleats

Apart from very simple gathered headings which really are not worth doing by hand, pencil pleats are the easiest to work and therefore the best for an absolute beginner to attempt. They are, in effect, only a deep gathered heading made by sewing two rows of large, evenly spaced stitches on the wrong side of the fabric with smaller stitches on the right side which, when gathered up, produce pencil pleats.

For this type of heading, the fabric width required is one and three-quarter times to twice the length of the track. The method is as follows:

(a) Make up the curtains in the usual way. Add the stiffener, fold in the lining at the top of the curtain and hem into position.

(b) Now here's where care and attention to detail show: to achieve crisp, professional pleats, spread the curtain out flat, wrong side uppermost, and draw two horizontal guide lines along the top and bottom edges of the stiffener. (Use tailor's chalk for this.) Then mark in vertical lines every 2 cm, joining the two horizontal lines. This simple trick will ensure your stitches match up exactly opposite each other, top and bottom, and thus your pleats will be straight and true.

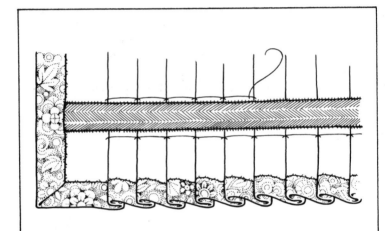

Fig. 14 Hand-made pencil pleats. The tape is hemstitched to the curtain to anchor the pleats and there is a line of lockstitch on either side of the tape for added security

(c) Take a long length of button thread and make two rows of stitches along each horizontal line. Use the vertical lines to match up your stitching and make each stitch approximately 1.5 cm on the wrong side and 0.5 cm on the right side of the curtain.

(d)   Draw up the threads to the final width of the curtain. Distribute the pleats evenly.

(e)   Cut a length of plain or pocketed non-drawing curtain tape, 3 cm wide, to the exact width of the finished curtain. Pin into position across the curtain, and turn in the ends. Oversew all round the tape by hand, catching each pleat to the tape to provide stability.

(f)   Lock the pleats above and below the tape to hold them firmly and give greater depth.

(g)   Stitch simple curtain hooks to the tape or, if it is pocketed, insert standard hooks or rings.

Pinch Pleats

Numerous charts and hundreds of hints have been published to help the novice curtain maker 'plot' hand-stitched pinch pleats. Most are confusing and some involve so much calculation that all but the most determined give up before they begin. But there is no need for the task to be so time-consuming.

The professional curtain maker's rule of thumb is ← **much easier: simply allow four pleats for every 122 cm width of fabric. Thus, if your curtain contains one and a half widths of fabric, you will need to introduce six pleats and five spaces.**

Now let's fix a formula to help you plot the pleats to fit your track exactly. The idea is to position them so that there is one pleat at each end with the remainder evenly placed along the track. This, in fact, involves some arithmetic, but not very much.

(a)   First, from your flat made-up curtain, subtract the width of the final heading. Remember to include the return to the wall and centre overlap. The amount you have left over is the *spare fabric* from which you make the pleats.

(b)   Then, to calculate the amount of material in each pleat, divide the spare fabric by the number of

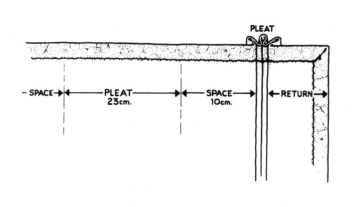

Fig. 15 How to plot pinch pleats, allowing four pleats per 122 cm width of fabric

pleats you wish to obtain — i.e., six, in a curtain made from one and a half widths of fabric.

(c) Lastly, position the spaces: lay the curtain out flat, mark off the return and overlap with tailor's chalk, and divide the remaining width of the curtain by the number of spaces. As we have seen, a one-and-a-half-widths curtain with six pleats will have five spaces. To find the measurement of each space, divide the final required heading width, less the return and overlap, by the number of spaces: thus, a curtain to cover an area of 50 cm has five spaces and each space measures 10 cm. This means your final curtain will have six pleats separated by five spaces of 10 cm each, plus a frontal overlap and a return to the wall.

To make the heading, use the following procedure. Your fabric width requirement will be two to two and a half times the length of the track.

(a) Make up the curtain in the usual way. Add the stiffener, fold in the lining at the top and hem into position.

(b)   Spread the curtain out flat. Measure and mark out, in this order, the return, a pleat followed by a space, followed by another pleat, and so on, across the curtain, finishing with a pleat before the central overlap.

(c)   Fold, pin, tack and then machine stitch single pleats into position from the top of the curtain to the base of the stiffener. This is done on the right side of the curtain. See Fig. 16.

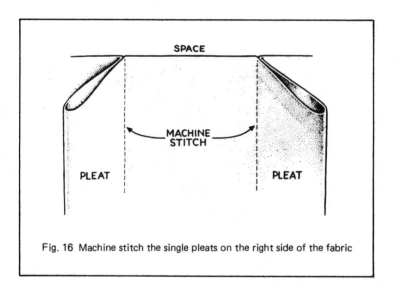

Fig. 16 Machine stitch the single pleats on the right side of the fabric

(d)   Also on the right side of the curtain, tuck two folds of material from the single pleat inwards to form the triple pleat. **Hand stitch through the pleat** ← **to hold it firmly in position. Further secure the pleats if necessary at the top with oversewing.**

(e)   Apply non-drawing curtain tape to the wrong side of the curtain. Hemstitch the tape into position all round. Sew curtain hooks on to the tape at regular intervals, making sure there is a hook behind each pleat.

If you prefer to make the increasingly popular goblet heading, plot and construct pleats as instructed above, but open the top of the pleats out to make a goblet shape and oversew the edge of each 'goblet' to the curtain on either side of the machine stitching (see Fig. 17).

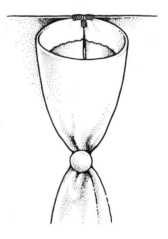

Fig. 17 Goblet pleat shaped by opening out a single pleat and oversewing the edge of each 'goblet' on either side of the machine stitching

To make this type of heading even more stunning, 'stuff' each 'goblet' with tissues or cotton wool and stitch a self-covered button at the base of each pleat.

Box Pleats

Box pleats make an attractive heading which can be used for lined or unlined valances as well as curtains. Once you master the art of marking out the fabric for the pleats, the rest is easy.

Your fabric width requirement in this case is three times the length of the track. For ease of calculation, **make your final width of fabric divisable by 10, 20 ←** **or 30 cm, i.e., the amount of fabric each pleat will require.**

The procedure for making a box-pleated heading by hand is:

(a)   Make up the curtain in the usual way. Add the stiffener, fold in the lining at the top and hem into position.

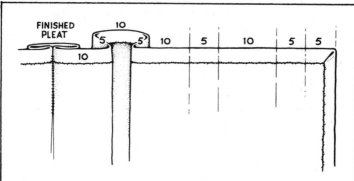

Fig. 18 How to plot and form a box pleat. The pleats are slipstitched together at the back

(b)   Lay the curtain out flat and measure and plot the pleats. To do this, make your first mark 5 cm in from the edge of the curtain, follow it with a further 5 cm, then mark 10-cm and 5-cm points alternately across the rest of the curtain, ending with two 5-cm spaces. This will allow you pleats of 10 cm with 10-cm spaces between each. The best depth to make these pleats is 8 cm.

(c)   To fold the pleats, begin at a point 20 cm in from the edge of the curtain and join this to the next point 20 cm further on. Pin, and tack the pleat into position. Leave a space of 10 cm and then join the next two 20-cm points together. Repeat the pattern across the curtain, finishing with the two 5-cm spaces. Finally, machine stitch the pleats on the right side of the fabric to a depth of 8 cm.

(d)   Form and flatten pleats on the right side of the fabric and secure with a few stitches. Press.

(e)   On the wrong side of the curtain, slipstitch the pleats together, taking the thread right through from the lining to the main fabric to prevent sagging.

(f)   Apply non-drawing tape to the wrong side of the curtain to help stabilize the pleats. (The tape must be hemmed into position all round.)

(g)   Sew ordinary brass curtain hooks on to the tape in the usual way, 2 cm in from each edge and behind each pleat across the curtain.

→ **(h)   For floor-length curtains, make a button hold bar at the base of all the pleats to retain their position the length of the curtain.**

Scalloped Heading

This type of heading is generally used for unlined cafe curtains at windows or to conceal shelves or doors. However, it can also look very attractive used on full-length curtains suspended from wooden poles. It is not difficult to make; the secret of success lies in selecting sufficiently firm fabric to show the scallops off to their full advantage. And the joy of a scalloped heading is that it requires far less fabric than most other types of hand-made heading.

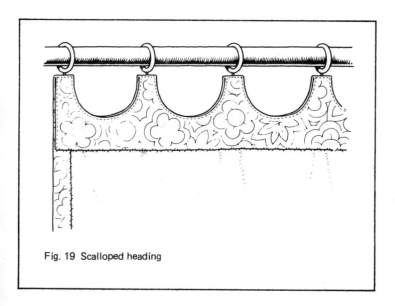

Fig. 19 Scalloped heading

The fabric width requirement for this type of heading is only one and a half times the length of the track.

Make a scalloped heading in the following way:

(a) Make up a stiff card template for the scallops first. (A scallop is really just a circle squared off at one end.) Draw round a saucer, tin lid or other circular object if you don't own a pair of compasses.

(b) Next, make a paper pattern of scallops to fit the finished curtain. **The quickest way to do this is to cut** ◄── **out a sheet of paper the width of the curtain. Fold it in equal sections, and then draw on it the shape of your desired scallop using the previously prepared template. Cut through all thicknesses of the paper and open out.** You now have a perfect paper pattern from which to make scalloped heading.

(c) Cut out and make up an unlined curtain. But do not hem the top edge or apply a heading tape.

(d) To make the scallops on the main fabric, fold over the top hem to the *right* side of the material. Pin and then tack the paper pattern to the turned-over hem. Be sure to tack in between each scallop. Machine stitch round the outline of each scallop.

(e)   Remove the paper pattern and cut away any unwanted fabric to make the scallops, but leave sufficient to make 1 cm turnings. Snip the turnings at the curved parts and clip the corners. Turn the hem right side out. Tuck in the raw edges and hem stitch to the wrong side of the curtain.

(f)   Attach curtain rings to the top of the straps of the scallops.

4 Nets and Sheers

Inner curtains of lace or muslin were first introduced in the nineteenth century. Today nets and sheers are an essential part of modern décor. Gleaming glass in a bare window may delight the modern architect, but it can be too much of a good thing in a home, particularly if you live in a town. Nets provide the necessary privacy in bedrooms and bathrooms, while full-length sheers help disguise ill-proportioned rooms, ungainly windows or depressing views.

Both net curtains and sheers are suited to home sewing. Straight machine stitching is quick and easy to do, while enthusiastic do-it-yourselfers' attention to detail ensures a professional finish which expensive shop-bought factory-made nets lack. Sewing your own nets means you can make allowances for uneven floors or oddly constructed windows and still save money.

If the golden rule for perfect window treatments is to use plenty of fabric, it is even more applicable when making nets and sheers. Both require at least three times the length of the track to look good, plus 2 cm hems on either side. However, there are some very open weave sheers now available which do *not* require side hems, and thus save time for the home curtain maker. Moreover, many nets and sheers, particularly those with patterned or lead-weighted hems, can be purchased in any width, again saving considerable time and temper, for there are no panels to stitch together and no patterns to match.

For sewing you will need: 100-per-cent synthetic thread, synthetic heading tape, a continental size 80 machine needle and some tissue paper. **Layers of fine** ←

fabric tend to slip while being seamed together. Avoid this by stitching the seam with a strip of tissue paper between the two layers of fabric. Once the seam is completed, the paper can be torn away.

The standard procedure for making up nets and sheers is very straightforward. Measure, cut out and hem up the sides and lower edge as for unlined curtains (see page 27). Make sure when you cut nets and sheers that you cut between a strong down thread so that small pieces of thread remain protruding horizontally. This helps the edge stay firm and free from fraying and allows a single hem in some cases.

Apply your chosen heading tape: a smocked heading looks good on nets; or perhaps your preference is for a simple cased heading which slots over a rod or wire.

Cased Heading

Allow 12 cm above the rod or wire when you measure for fabric. Make up the curtain as usual, but at the top turn over and tack a double 6-cm hem. Machine stitch in place with two lines of stitching 2.4 cm apart. Measure your first line of stitching 2.5 cm from the top of the curtain to provide sufficient heading above the rod.

Cross-over Curtains

This style of curtaining is often made from net or other transparent Terylene fabric sold by the metre with a ready-made frill down each side. However, there is a snag about using this type of fabric: when you come to cut out the curtains, there will be no frill along the lower sloping edge! It is advisable, therefore, to buy plain, less expensive fabric and make your own frill. Each panel should be two to three times the width of the track, and you must remember to purchase sufficient additional fabric to make the frill.

To make up cross-over curtains, proceed as follows:

(a) Cut out the fabric as shown in Fig. 20 and make a narrow hem along the sloping edge.

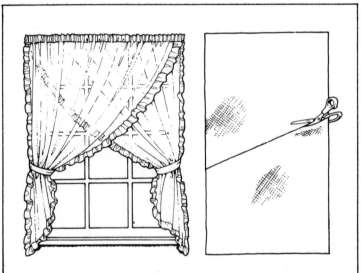

Fig. 20 Cross-over curtains. The fabric is cut diagonally to avoid wastage, and the heading tape is applied to each end, i.e. to the edges opposite the two sloping ones

(b) Make up a narrow frill, long enough to fit to three sides of each curtain.

The simplest way to gather a frill is to stitch a simple drawing tape along the wrong side of a narrow strip of fabric and draw up to the required length. Knot the ends and arrange the gathers evenly.

(c) Fit the frill to the curtains and pin in position. Machine stitch the frill into position.

(d) Apply a simple heading tape to each curtain. Draw up, insert hooks and **arrange with an overlap on a double-rod curtain set specifically made for this type of window treatment.**

5 Top Treatments: Pelmets, Valances, Swags and Tails

Stiffened pelmets, often teamed with an elaborately draped valance, were popular in the great houses of the eighteenth century. Before that, curtains were suspended from rods set behind carved wooden pelmets, placed over portiers (doorways), windows or beds. With the advent of better housing, smaller rooms and more adequate heating in the nineteenth century, bed hangings became lighter and less numerous, while pelmets and valances carried less ornamentation. Later still, in the 1960s and 70s, commercially made curtain heading tapes brought pinch and pencil pleats within the scope of many DIY home decorators. Pelmets and valances lost favour and, sadly, were almost forgotten. Today, however, both are back in fashion, and it is easy to understand why.

For a start, a stiffened pelmet gives just the right touch of formality to a traditional room; while a frilled or pleated valance provides a soft and gentle appearance suitable for bedrooms or a country cottage. Both have the advantage of hiding the curtain track and heading. Both ensure economy — you need only a simple, inexpensive drawing tape, and the fabric width requirement is just one and a half times the length of the track. Both are easy and quite quick to make at home — most of the work can be completed with an ordinary sewing machine and a tube of glue. And both can be taken down for dry-cleaning.

What is the difference between a pelmet and a valance? Very little — the two are frequently confused in casual conversation. The real answer lies in their construction and hanging. A stiffened pelmet is made from a straight piece of shaped fabric attached to a pelmet board. (A pelmet board is fitted like a shelf across the window reveal; detailed instructions for fitting are given below.) A valance, on the other hand, is usually ruched, frilled or pleated and hung from a rod or track projecting above the window. In essence a valance is a small, very short curtain and is made in almost exactly the same way.

Making a Pelmet Board

Before you can begin to make a stiffened-fabric pelmet, you must have a pelmet board to support the pelmet. You may have been lucky enough to inherit one fixed in position, but if not, it is a simple matter to make one yourself. Here's how:

(a) Consider the position of your proposed pelmet and window treatment. Pelmets can be either recessed into the window frame or made to project away from the frame.

(b) Measure up and make the pelmet board exactly like a shelf. See Fig. 21. Use 1-cm-thick plywood or hardwood and buy angle irons for fixing. Pelmet boards are normally made 10 cm deep and extend 5 to 7 cm beyond the length of the track – i.e., 2.5 cm each end to allow for turning the pelmet fabric and for access to fit runners and hang curtains.

(c)   Fix the pelmet board as follows:

For recessed curtains, position the angle irons so that the pelmet board will lie flush with the inner edge of the beading of the window frame. Screw the angle irons into the back of the board and to the upper surface of the reveal.

For a projecting pelmet, attach the angle irons to the wall above the window and position and fix the pelmet board as you would a shelf.

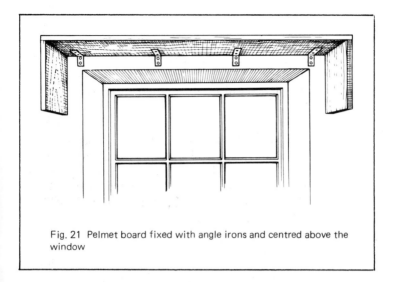

Fig. 21 Pelmet board fixed with angle irons and centred above the window

Remember that the board must project 10 cm ← away from the wall to allow clearance for both the track and the pulled-back curtains. It is easy to forget how very bulky curtains can be when drawn back.

Making a Pelmet

Pelmets can be made from wood and painted to match the window frame, or from stiffened fabric stretched across a pelmet board.

The wooden variety is readily available from specialist shops or can be made at home. It is also possible to apply padded upholstery work directly to a wooden pelmet. However, the snag about this type of top treatment is that it cannot be laundered or dry-cleaned.

Stiffened-fabric pelmets make a practical and attractive alternative. They are much easier to work at home and can be satisfactorily taken down for dry-cleaning. Usually they are made from the same type of material as the curtains, mounted on to stiff buckram and trimmed with braid or a fringe.

Making your own pelmets can be a satisfying and rewarding task. Results are speedy, and working with fabric, glue and braid is fun — little or no stitching is required.

First, choose a shape for your pelmet: straight, curved, scalloped, what you will. Draw a rough sketch, bearing in mind that the depth of your pelmet must be in proportion to the curtains — allow approximately 4 cm for every 30 cm of curtain drop. **The professional rule of thumb is to allow one-sixth of the total depth for floor-length curtains.**

Next, look carefully at the design and ask yourself the following questions:

(a)   Does the point at which the curtains will hang, when drawn back, form the start of the end sections in your design? It must, because the end sections and returns must be made to the same depth.

(b)   Does the shallowest part of the pelmet cover the track or rail? Obviously no one wants to see the fittings!

(c)   If the design is for a scalloped edge, have you measured the pattern on the fabric — if there is one — and considered how it will fit in with your design? If your fabric is difficult to match, perhaps a less complicated design would be better.

Once you are satisfied with your design, it is sensible to make a template. Find a newspaper larger than the desired size of the pelmet. Fold it in half widthwise and draw out your design, starting from the centre and using object(s) which are readily available, e.g., household plates, as guides to draw round where necessary. Cut round your drawing, open out the paper pattern, centre and then pin on the pelmet board to see how it looks. It is a good idea to leave your pattern in place for two or three days to make quite sure it is exactly right.

When the design is finalized, you are in a position

to estimate fabric requirements. First, measure the length of the pelmet board, including the two 10-cm returns at each end and adding on 5 cm for turnings. This measurement will give you the overall width of the fabric required. Next, measure the depth of your paper pattern and add 10 cm for turnings.

Remember: most windows are more than 122 cm wide, the usual fabric width, and a pelmet with a centre seam is to be avoided at all costs. **To overcome** ← **the problem, centre one width of fabric with the middle of the pelmet pattern and add the necessary extra fabric to each side of this width.**

You also need: lining and interlining, a piece of buckram (cut to the design of the pelmet), braid, cords, piping and possibly a tube of fabric glue.

There are two ways to construct a pelmet. The question is whether you prefer to stick or sew — both techniques are equally satisfactory and easy to use. Here's the 'stick' method because, for my money, it's not just the quickest; it's also the best.

(a) Cut out the materials as follows: the buckram exactly to your paper pattern; the lining and main fabric out 10 cm larger and wider than the paper; the interlining, i.e., the bump or domette, to only 5 cm wider than the paper pattern.

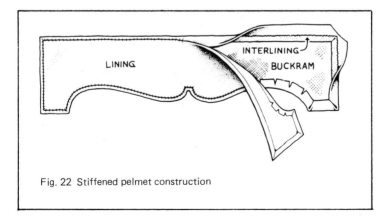

Fig. 22 Stiffened pelmet construction

(b)   Centre the shaped buckram over the interlining. Dampen the edges of the buckram slightly for about 2 cm all round. Fold the interlining over the buckram and then steam press into position. (The damp heat releases the glue incorporated into the buckram which provides stiffening. However, if this proves inadequate, add a dab of glue.) Start at the top, continue on round the pelmet, slash all concave curves, and cut away any surplus fabric on the convex curves.
(c)   Lay the main fabric on a table, wrong side up. Cover with the interlining and buckram. Lay the interlining against the main fabric. Fold the main fabric over the buckram. Dampen as before and steam press into position — slipstitch the corners.

If your fabric is particularly sheer or you prefer to use the stitch method, attach the interlining/buckram/lining in the same way as described for tie-backs (see page 39).
(d)   Apply any decorative trimming to the right side of the main fabric at this stage. Do this with stabstitches from the front of the pelmet through the buckram to the wrong side.
(e)   Place the lining in position over the buckram. Fold in the turnings and slipstitch all round.

Fixing a Pelmet

A pelmet may be fixed to the pelmet board in various ways. The simplest method is to tack it in place with gimp pins and then, if necessary, cover the line of gimp pins with braid. **Alternatively, use Velcro — one strip is stitched to the pelmet and the other stapled (with a staple gun) to the pelmet board.**

Making a Valance

A valance gives a soft, informal look to curtains. It may be simply gathered or pleated. While a gathered valance needs no stiffening, it is usually lined and finished with plain heading tape. **More elaborate** ← **pleated headings, best made with the aid of a commercial heading tape, must be stiffened with interlining** and the tape positioned 5 cm from the top of the strip of fabric to prevent sagging.

When estimating fabric requirements, remember that the depth of the completed valance is calculated

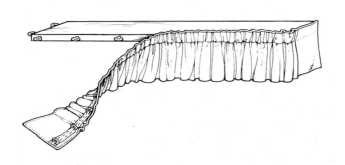

Fig. 23 Gathered valance with heading tape and curtain hooks. In this case the valance is attached to the pelmet board by hooks which slot through screw eyes. A curtain track or valance rail may be used with equal effect

in exactly the same way as that of a pelmet. The width of the fabric is estimated in the same way as for curtains, i.e., depending on the chosen heading. The length of the fabric required is equal to the depth of the finished valance, plus allowances for hem and heading.

You also need: the same amount of lining as main fabric, interlining for stiffening, curtain tape to choice, and hooks. **One professional curtain maker known to the author advocates the use of 'smocking' heading tapes for valances, and very effective they look.**

The procedure to follow when making a valance is:

(a) Cut out and join together any necessary widths of the main fabric, lining and interlining. Place the main fabric wrong side up. Position the interlining over the main fabric and lock into position.

(b) Lock the lining to the interfacing. Leave 14 cm unstitched at the top of the valance and 15 cm at the bottom for turnings.

(c) Turn in the hem allowances all round the valance and slipstitch the lining to the main fabric as described for lined curtains (see page 29).

(d) Apply your chosen heading tape — insert hooks and draw up to the required width or make a hand-pleated heading.

To mount the valance, suspend it from either a valance rail — if you have one — or from eyelet holes screwed into a pelmet board.

For an extra-simple unlined valance — suitable for a kitchen or bathroom — make a deep hem and thread through a casing a rod or wire.

Swags and Tails

These are formal headings for curtains which depend for their grace and elegance upon clever draping. Although not often attempted by the amateur curtain maker, they are not particularly difficult to tackle. The key to success lies in choosing the right sort of soft, supple material and in carrying out some careful preparation before you begin work on the main fabric.

It is also important to realize that both swags and tails, because of their many folds, use a great deal of material. Budget accordingly! And because draping is a skilled business, be wise and invest in some butter muslin or other inexpensive fabric with which to practise before you attempt the exercise in earnest.

How to Make a Swag

Swags have a definite shape and form and must be individually pleated up. Shapes vary according to the size and effect required and sadly there are no ready-made pleating tapes to aid the making process. However, the average pattern shown (see Fig. 24) can be adapted to suit most window treatments.

To make a swag, the method is as follows:

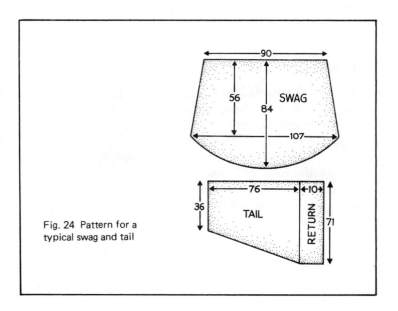

Fig. 24 Pattern for a typical swag and tail

(a) Measure, rule and cut out a paper pattern.

(b) Cut out the 'practice fabric' to match the paper pattern.

(c) Fold and press in 2.5-cm turnings on all sides of the fabric.

(d) Tack and pleat up sides, the two shortest sides,

73

opposite each other, to form a pretty curve. Do not worry if you fail to get both even on the first attempt. Draping swags is a knack which requires practice.

(e)   Once you obtain a satisfactory prototype and feel confident, cut out and pleat up the main fabric and stitch the pleats securely into position.

→ (f)   **Cut the lining to the same size as the now completed swag, plus 2.5 cm for turnings.** Do not cut the lining to match the original pattern.

(g)   Seam the lining to the top edge of the swag. Fold in the lining turnings and slipstitch the remaining sides of the swag together.

(h)   Centre and fix the swag to a pelmet board with tacks or gimp pins.

How to Make a Tail

You need two tails for each window treatment, one on each side of the centrally placed swag. The procedure is as follows:

(a)   Decide on a design or adapt the one shown in Fig. 25 to suit your windows. Then measure the width, the long side and the short side. Make a paper pattern with the measurements.

(b)   Cut out the fabric and lining to match the paper pattern. Allow 2.5 cm turnings all round.

(c)   Lay the main fabric, right side down, on a table and position the lining on top. Tuck in the turnings all round. Pin, press and slipstitch the fabric and the lining together.

(d)   If using the measurements shown in Fig. 25, pleat up the tail vertically to give a pleated width of 15 cm. Leave a 10-cm return at the long side. Stitch in the pleats across the top of the tail only. You want them to fan out a little when hung.

(e)   Place the tail into position over the swag and fold the outer edge just over the pelmet board. Remember to place the return round the far side of the pelmet board. Fix into position with gimp pins or tacks.

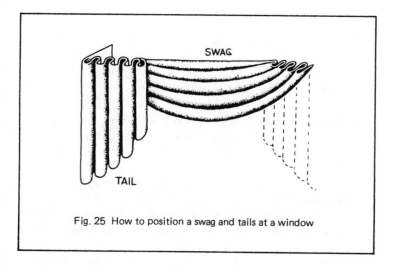

Fig. 25 How to position a swag and tails at a window

6 Blinds

Blinds are an increasingly popular form of window treatment. They are practical: light can be admitted or shut out in a trice. They are inexpensive: fabric requirements are only a fraction of those needed for traditional curtaining. Above all, they offer a useful and attractive way to cope with 'awkward' windows.

There are three basic types of blind and all three can be satisfactorily made at home with a little help from the following pages. The three main styles are: roller blinds, the tried, trusted, practical way to treat functional windows; festoon blinds, a frivolous and frankly feminine form of window covering; and Roman blinds, the perfect complement to crisp, no-nonsense decor in a modern setting.

The important differences between a festoon blind and a Roman blind are: a Roman blind is lined while a festoon blind is left unlined; and for Roman blinds the vertical tapes are *not* gathered up and thus, when down, the blind fits smoothly to the window.

Roller Blinds

Ten years ago roller blinds had to be specially ordered from various commercial firms and fitted by experts — an exhausting, time-consuming and costly process. Today there are so many kits available in the shops that making and fitting your own roller blinds at home in an evening is a relatively easy and inexpensive task.

What makes roller blinds so practical? To begin with, they can be trimmed to fit almost any awkwardly shaped window, e.g., a dormer. **They can be backed with black fabric to shut out unwelcome morning**

light. And they can be decorated, trimmed or edged to suit your decor. Used in conjunction with dress curtains (which do not draw − the blind covers the naked window) they help cut the cost of curtaining. And they are extremely easy to keep clean.

Measuring Up and Materials

Consider first your choice of fabric. Roller blinds must be made from light, fairly stiff, closely woven material. Fabric with a loose weave may stretch with time and make your blind 'wavy'; while thick fabrics, right from the start, will not roll satisfactorily.

Specially prepared roller blind fabrics sold in various widths up to 183 cm are the best bet for the novice blind maker. They are available in a variety of colours and patterns from most department stores and provide an almost instant professional finish. They require no stiffening treatment. There is no danger of fraying edges − thus no need for side hems. And they repel both dust and dirt, have a fade-resistant finish, and can be easily sponged clean.

However, it is perfectly possible to use other types of furnishing fabric providing the material undergoes a stiffening process and, of course, that it is of a suitable weave. Special fabric stiffeners to strengthen cloth can be bought in aerosol cans or a liquid form. **When you use stiffener from an aerosol can, be sure** ← **to spray both sides of the fabric. If you choose a liquid stiffener, either paint it over the material or dip the fabric into the liquid.**

PVC or plastic-backed fabrics, which need no stiffening, may also be used for roller blinds and make a practical choice for kitchens and bathrooms where condensation may be a problem and frequent cleaning a necessity.

Your next step is to decide whether the blind is to be fixed inside or outside the window recess. Take exact measurements and do use a metal metre rule, not a cloth tape, because even the smallest slip can prevent a smooth fit.

To estimate the amount of fabric required, make the width of the fabric equal to the measurement of the trimmed roller and the length of the blind 30 cm longer than your required drop. This extra 30 cm is sufficient for the roller to remain covered when the blind is pulled down, and for the bottom hem.

Besides the fabric, you also need a roller blind kit. This consists of:

1   One wooden roller to be trimmed to an exact fit. The roller has a spring and metal cap with rectangular pin at one end. A second metal cap with a rounded end is also provided to fit on to the bare end of the roller once it has been trimmed to your requirements.

2   Two brackets for fixing the roller blind to the window frame.

3   Tacks to attach the blind fabric to the roller.

4   A wooden batten or lath to slip through the hem to keep the blind straight.

5   Cord holder and acorn, or half-handle for drawing.

Making Up

To make up a roller blind, proceed as follows:

(a) Fix the brackets. Follow the manufacturer's instructions and double-check that you mount the bracket for the square pin on the left-hand side of the window and that for the round pin on the right.

(b) Trim the roller to fit exactly between the two brackets. Fit the metal cap and round pin provided to the bare, trimmed end of the roller and hammer home.

(c) Cut the fabric to the exact size of the prepared roller. Use a T-square or table edge to ensure an accurate result. But before you launch out with the scissors, look over the fabric and position any pattern or designs with care.

(d) At the lower edge of the blind, turn up the fabric 1 cm. Press. Turn up a further 4 cm and machine stitch the hem into position. Slide the batten or lath into the pocket thus formed.

For blinds with a decorative edge, make the lath tuck further up the blind.

(e) Attach the fabric to the roller — more easily said than done! The trick here is to stop the fabric slipping about while you apply the tacks. To do this, **place the fabric on a table, right side up. Lay the ←— roller across the top of the fabric with the square pin on the left-hand side. Turn the fabric over 1 cm and stick to the roller along the guide line with self-adhesive tape. With the fabric firmly in place, it is an easy matter to hammer home the pins provided.**

(f) Insert the cord into the cord holder. Screw the holder into place on the wrong side of the blind. Slot the loose end of the cord through the acorn and knot.

(g) Roll up the blind carefully by hand and slot into the brackets — square pin into the left-hand bracket, round pin into the right.

(h) Adjust the tension by pulling the blind down as far as it will go. If further tension is required, remove the blind from the brackets, roll up again by hand, reinsert between the brackets and pull down. Be careful not to over-tension.

Remember also these tips: be certain your blind is assembled the correct way round; never put oil on the spring roller; and always use the cord to pull the blind up and down.

Decoration and Trimming

There are many interesting ways to trim a roller blind easily and with little extra cost. Some fabrics lend themselves to a cut-out design with a brass rod pushed through the bottom instead of a wooden batten. Another idea is to shape the bottom edge beneath the batten into scallops. Or you can simply add a fringe or braid.

To Make a Scalloped or Other Cut-out Edge

In addition to the regular roller blind kit you need:

1   Extra fabric to accommodate the scallops (add to the usual drop measurement *twice* the amount of the required scallop depth)
2   A strip of buckram
3   Clear glue
4   Stiff cardboard

This is what you do:

(a)   Begin to make up the blind as usual. Fit to the roller, but do not make the pocket for the lath.

(b)   Make up a template from the cardboard. Use a pair of compasses, a saucer or round tin as a guide. Be sure that the design fits evenly on the width of the blind so that the scallops or points are equal on each side of the blind.

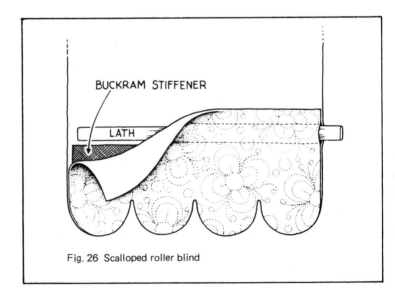

Fig. 26 Scalloped roller blind

(c) Fold back approximately 13 to 15 cm of fabric at the bottom to the back of the blind. Crease and press along the fold. Open out the flap made by the crease and cut a piece of buckram the same width as the blind but 4 cm shorter than the flap.

Apply clear glue to both sides of the buckram and ← **place into the pressed crease. Fold over the flap on to the buckram and press the three layers together firmly. Allow to dry.**

On no account allow glue to slip on to the 4 cm of ← **fabric not covered by buckram.**

(d) Once the glue is quite dry, make the pocket for the lath from the remaining 4-cm overlap by sewing two rows of machine stitching.

(e) Lay the template on the front, folded, glued fabric with the lower bottom scalloped edge exactly on the crease. Mark round the curves and then cut out.

(f) The scalloped edge may be overlocked by machine stitching if you feel industrious, but it is not really necessary if the fabric has been satisfactorily glued together.

(g) Place the lath in the prepared pocket. Apply the cord holder.

(h) Trim the edges with plain braid, tassel, fringing or bobble fringe – all can be glued into position. Add a fringed or tassel pull instead of an acorn to complete the picture.

Cut-out Edges with a Brass Batten

Proceed as before and make a paper pattern. Remember to allow extra blind fabric for the edging. Mark an allowance – 4 cm wide – for the batten casing at the bottom of the fold. Add the buckram and glue the fabric together from the top, but be sure to leave the bottom batten allowance free from glue. Cut out the reversed tabs or scallops. Machine stitch the batten casing top and bottom. Slot in the brass rod and hang.

Festoon Blinds

This type of blind is best made with lightweight fabric which will ruche gracefully and fall into soft, puffy folds — it will give a luxurious appearance to a bedroom or bathroom.

Although from the front festoon blinds may look complicated, fear not: the operational mechanism is very simple. Their secret lies in the rows of rings

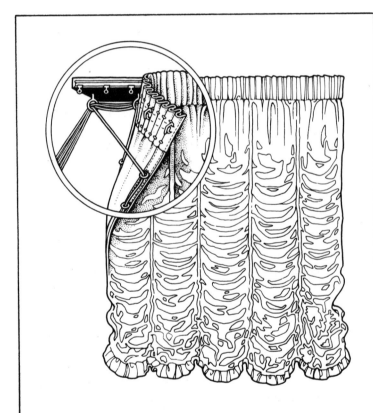

Fig. 27 Festoon blind with pencil-pleated heading and vertical gathering tapes

attached to the back of the blind through which cords are threaded to pull the blind up or let it down. And it is the raising of the blind, together with the vertical application of gathering tape, which produces the deep, ballooning folds.

Measuring Up and Materials

First decide how many scallops are to be included in the blind. Next, consider the function of the blind. Will it be left down permanently or partially drawn up to show off the luxurious swags? Do you wish to ruche the blind all over? This will, of course, involve using more fabric. Finally, are you keen to add a frill around the edges or along the lower hem?

Once the above points have been settled, use the following guide to help you sort out the fabric requirements.

Width You need double the width of the window, plus 3 cm extra for side hems. If widths of fabric have to be joined together to achieve the correct blind width, allow a further 3 cm for French seams.

Length For a straightforward festoon blind which will be raised to some extent over the window, you need one and a half times the length of the window plus 20 cm for hems. For an extravagantly full ruched blind, allow two and a half times the length of the window plus 20 cm for turnings.

You also need: a plywood heading board approximately 2.5 to 5 cm wide, cut to the width of the blind; a curtain track cut to the same length; two or three angle irons for fixing the heading board to the window frame; several screw eyes; non-stretch cord and a brass cleat to hold the blind cords in place; heading tape; simple gathering tape; small plastic split curtain rings; and standard curtain hooks.

Making Up

(a) Cut out the fabric. Join together any necessary widths. Hem the sides and lower edge. Make and attach the frill if required. Look at Fig. 28 for clarification of the rest of the instructions.

→ (b) **Lay the blind out flat, wrong side up. Mark in with chalk the positions for the vertical tapes. These should be placed down each side and at regular**

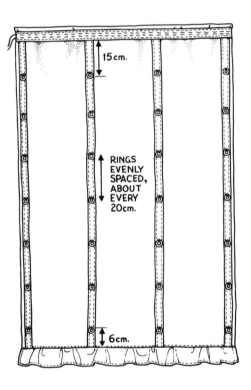

Fig. 28 How to assemble a festoon blind. Mark in and stitch down the tapes. Apply the rings at regular intervals

intervals across the body of the blind — approximately **20 cm apart.** Do not worry if the intervals between the tapes appear huge. Remember the distance between the tapes is at least double that of the finished swag, because at this point the blind is twice the width of the window!

(c)   Cut, pin and machine stitch simple drawing tapes into position down the vertical guide lines. Insert split rings at regular intervals approximately 20 cm apart along each tape. Place the first split ring 15 cm from the top of the blind and the last 7 cm up from the bottom hem. Make sure all the rings are parallel.

(d)   Apply the heading tape, draw up the blind to fit the width of the window and knot the cords. Draw the vertical tapes up to the required length of the blind and knot the cords. Distribute the gathered fabric evenly in both cases.

(e)   Cut lengths of cord (one for each vertical row of split rings) to measure twice the length of the blind and once the width. Lay the blind out flat, tie one cord to the first ring at the bottom of each and then thread up vertically through the lines of rings.

(f)   Mount the curtain track in the front of the heading board. Position and insert the screw eyes into the under side of the board, parallel to the vertical rows of tape and rings.

(g)   Hang the completed blind on the curtain track. Then, working from the left edge of the blind, thread the first cord through the screw eye on the board immediately above the tape and continue to thread the cord on to the right through each screw eye. Repeat the stringing for each tape. Knot all the cords together approximately 3 cm from the right outside edge of the blind. **Use a larger screw eye on the far** ← **right of the blind to accommodate all the cords.**

Fix the heading board, complete with track and blind, to the window frame with angle irons.

(h)   Cut the cords at the lower edge of the blind,

then plait and knot them together. Fix a cleat to the window reveal. To raise the blind, pull the cords and wind the slack round the brass cleat.

Roman Blinds

Roman blinds draw up to the top of a window in neat pleats. They are incredibly easy to make and work on much the same principle as festoon blinds, i.e., they are drawn up on cords threaded through rings and suspended from a wooden heading board.

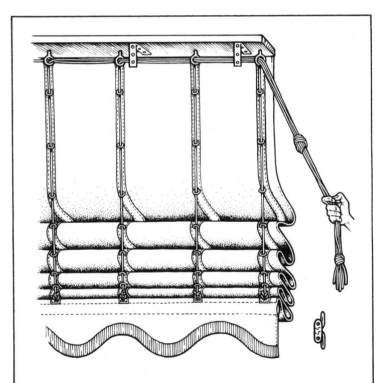

Fig. 29 A Roman blind, showing the construction with vertical tapes, cords threaded through evenly spaced rings, and heading board

For best results choose a sturdy fabric and good-quality lining — the most suitable combination to provide sufficient body for the blind to fold easily and hang plumb.

Measuring Up and Materials

Measure the width and length of the window and calculate the fabric requirement as follows:

Width You need the measured width of the window plus 3 cm for side turnings.

Length To the length of the window add 15 cm for top and bottom hems — 7.5 cm each.

You also need: a plywood heading board approximately 2.5 to 5 cm wide cut to the width of the blind; two or three angle irons for fixing the board to the window frame; screw eyes; non-stretch cord; simple drawing tape, split curtain rings; a metal rod the width of the blind; and a cleat to hold the cords in place.

Making Up

(a) Cut out the main fabric and lining. Seam together any necessary widths.

(b) Place the right side of the main fabric against the right side of the lining. Pin into position and machine stitch down both sides and along the lower edge, just as you would when making a bag. Turn fabrics right sides out and press.

(c) Mark in two parallel guide lines across the lower edge of the blind for the metal rod. Make the first line 10 cm up from the bottom of the blind and the second 5 cm up from that.

(d) Mark in guide lines for the vertical tapes 15 cm from each outer edge and every 15 cm across the body of the blind. Pin simple drawing tapes on each vertical guide line and machine stitch into position.

Begin each line from the metal rod guide line. Stitch through *both* the main fabric and the lining.

(e) At the top of the blind turn in the raw edges of the lining and main fabric, tuck in the ends of tape and machine stitch across the blind.

(f) Machine stitch along the metal rod casing guide lines. Unpick the necessary side hem at one end and insert the metal rod. Slipstitch the two sides together again.

(g) Insert the split rings into the vertical tapes. Make the first ring 15 cm from the top of the metal batten. As with festoon blinds, it is essential that you place the rings at regular intervals and that they are evenly spaced and parallel.

(h) Arrange the screw eyes on the underside of the heading board. Make sure each screw eye is placed exactly opposite each vertical row of rings on the blind. You need a slightly larger screw eye on the far right side of the board to help bear the weight of all the drawing cords. Tack the blind to the heading board.

(i) Cut lengths of cord twice the length of the blind plus once the width. Lay the blind flat out and tie one cord to each bottom ring. Thread the cords up through the rings to the screw eyes and on through each screw eye from left to right. Knot all the cords together 3 cm from the outer edge of the blind.

(j) Fix the heading board with the attached blind to the top of the window with two angle irons. Position the cleat on the window frame to hold the cords when the blind is drawn up.

(k) Cut the cords to make them level. Plait and knot together and add a decorative tassel for a fully finished effect.

7 Trimmings and Small Touches

Trimmings chosen with care add your individual signature to curtains — and the whole room. Sadly, to many people trimmings are synonymous with visions of fussy, over-elaborate, Edwardian interiors. In fact, they are a vital part of curtain design and the secret of success lies in choosing the right trimming for the right fabric and setting. There are no hard-and-fast rules about suitability, and if in doubt, be guided by your natural taste. However, there are a few pitfalls worth avoiding. So here are a few hints to help you choose wisely.

The range of trimmings available is extensive. Most are sold by the metre from soft-furnishing stores or in small specialist trimming shops in London or other big cities. Measure carefully and buy only sufficient for your needs; good trimmings are expensive.

Remember that the choice of trimming must be in keeping with the purpose of your curtains. If, for example, your curtains are washable, make sure the trimming is too. Another point is that the weight of the trimming should be in unison with that of the fabric.

Always choose trimming by daylight and match it ◄ **with a sample of your curtain material.** An inspired guess in artificial light will almost certainly lead to an expensive mistake.

Check that the heading on your chosen trimming has a firm finish and that the yarns of the 'skirt', e.g., the fringe, are even.

Finally, hand sew on all trimming unless you are perfectly sure that you, and your machine, can keep an absolutely straight line; wavy deviations will be very obvious once the curtains are hung. **Whichever method you choose, chalk a guide line on the main fabric before you begin to apply any trimming.**

Below is a list of eight common types of trimming and where to use them. Many different styles are available from your local soft-furnishing store, so make a couple of exploratory expeditions before you buy.

Silk ribbon An expensive and deliciously extravagant way to trim a plain silk fabric.

Rayon or polyester ribbon A less expensive but very acceptable substitute for silk ribbon.

Chenille bobble fringe This has a woolly texture but is, in fact, made from cotton. It looks great on cotton drapes and swags, or even a pelmet.

Cotton or silk cord An excellent trimming for tie-backs, or it can be used equally effectively as a border.

Lightweight nylon fringe Excellent for edging washable curtains, bedspreads or dressing-table curtains because it dries very quickly.

Rayon or other synthetic braid This looks great on glossy, glazed cottons. Some types of braid can be bought in a natural colour and then dyed to pick out a particular colour in the curtain pattern.

Silk tassel fringe For the really sumptuous look on very grand fabrics like velvet, brocade or polyester mixture.

Cotton ruching Provides a fresh finish for cottons and linens. Ideal for kitchens and bathrooms.

Heavy cotton fringe Comes in any width. Use very broad widths to trim heavy curtains at long windows.

Covered buttons Many soft-furnishing stores offer a button-covering service for customers who provide their own material. Keen do-it-yourselfers can buy metal buttons from haberdashery counters and make their own. However, the results obtained from heavy fabrics, e.g., velvet, are unlikely to prove satisfactory.

Piping

Piping is made by covering plain white cord with a chosen fabric. It gives a simple, distinguished look to both pelmets and tie-backs and can easily be made at home, providing you own a sewing machine.

The type of cord used to make piping is available in various sizes and materials. Selection and choice depend upon where and how the piping is to be used. Small, short curtains are best decorated with a fine piping. Large pelmets over full-length curtains can accommodate a more substantial style of piping. Try to buy shrink-resistant cord if possible. Shrinkage in the wash or at the dry-cleaners will make your once-perfect piping pucker. **If you cannot find shrink-** ←
resistant cord, shrink the ordinary sort yourself. Here's how: place the cord in a pan of boiling water and allow to simmer for three or four minutes. Drain and dry well before use.

How to Make and Apply Piping

(a)   Cut strips of bias from the main fabric. **The best** ←
way to find a bias grain (i.e., 'on the cross') is to fold the raw edge of the fabric across the grain of the fabric parallel to the selvedge. This line is the bias line; so for bias strips, cut parallel to the folded line. Your strips need to be approximately 4 cm wide.

(b)   Join the bias strips together on the straight grain of the fabric. To do this, place the strips together with the right sides facing upwards and machine stitch the seam, making sure that the strips form a 'V'.

(c)   Place the bias strips, wrong side up, on a table and lay the cord down the centre. Draw the two edges of the fabric together to enclose the cord. Pin

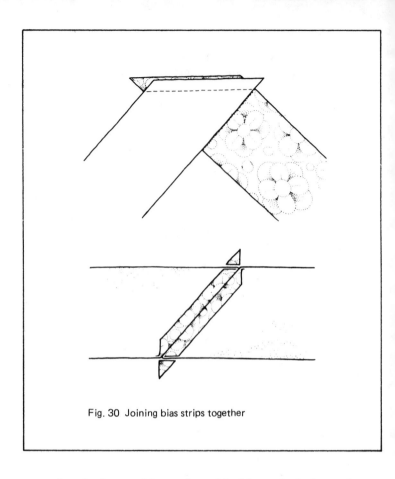

Fig. 30 Joining bias strips together

and tack the cord into place. Machine stitch down the strip of piping as close to the cord as possible. Use the piping foot attachment on your machine.

(d) Apply the cord by stitching the raw edges of the piping seam into the main seam of the fabric, i.e., stitch two pieces of main fabric together with the piping sandwiched in between them.

If the cord should need to be joined, unravel the two ends for a couple of centimetres. Trim each of the three strands, making the cord different lengths, and then retwist the two sets together and stitch into

92

position. This way you avoid any ugly lumps or bumps in your finished piping.

How to Apply Braid

The important thing to remember when applying ← braid is that you mark in a guide line, on the right side of the main fabric, before you begin to stitch. Be assured that attempts to save time and short cut this first step are doomed to produce poor results, and plenty of bad temper — do not be tempted to make do with 'just pins'.

The procedure for applying braid is as follows:

(a)   Mark in a guide line.
(b)   Centre the braid on the line, pin and then tack it into place.
(c)   Machine stitch the braid into position. If you are using a narrow braid, machine down the centre along its length. Wider braid must be machine stitched, or slipstitched by hand, all along both edges.

Check the tension on your machine before starting ← to ensure that the stitches are not pulled too tightly or the braid will pucker.

How to Apply Decorative Cord

Cord in various widths and a host of interesting shades is readily available from most soft-furnishing stores. It has the great advantage of being a lot less expensive than braid and can be applied to decorate curtains in exactly the same way. Cord can also be stitched to the edge of the curtain. Here's how:

(a)   Bind the end of the cord with thread to prevent it unravelling.
(b)   Since it is impossible to pin cord in position before you begin to stitch, to obtain satisfactory results place the cord on the edge of the right side of ←

the curtain with your left hand and continue to use this hand to control and guide the cord as you sew.

(c)   Use a matching button thread and stitch strands from the back of the cord into the folded edge of the curtain. Be sure the cord is firmly but not too tightly attached.

(d)   When you reach a corner, twist the cord slightly to make a neat turn and when you come to finish off, allow 2 or 3 cm extra, knot the cord in two places and cut in between them — a precaution against un-ravelling.

(e)   Finally, take the cord to the wrong side of the curtain, slip it under the lining and stitch down.

8 Sewing Section

Most straightforward stitching on curtains is done by
machine for both speed and strength. However, to
give curtains the smooth, professional look it is also
necessary to master a few special types of seam and
hand-sewing skills. None of the techniques mentioned
in this book are complicated, and the average reader
will probably already know most of them. But for all
absolute beginners, non-sewers and cases of total
amnesia, the following pages have been written to
guide you gently through the simple techniques
needed to make your curtains look professional.

Stitches

In all cases except when tacking, secure the end of
your thread with a couple of small stitches on top of
each other.

Tacking

Tacking is a temporary seam used to hold pieces of
fabric in place while the permanent stitching is being
done. It is normally worked from right to left.

Choose a brightly coloured thread which can be
easily and quickly distinguished. Start by securing
the thread with a knot and make stitches approximately 1 cm long and 1 cm apart. Finish with a back
stitch. Tack where the permanent stitching is to be
placed, and remove the tack stitches once the permanent work is in position — hence the brightly coloured
thread. Tacking is sometimes called 'basting' by the
trade.

→ Instead of using equal stitches, some professional curtain makers take two smaller stitches of perhaps 1 cm each and then one extra-long stitch of, say, 2.5 cm for added strength and speed when joining lengths of fabric together.

Hemming

This stitch is normally worked from right to left on the wrong side of the fabric. It is used to hold a folded edge to a flat fabric and the object of the exercise is to make sure that no stitches are visible on the right side of the material.

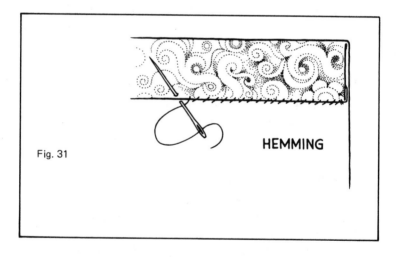

Fig. 31

HEMMING

First, position the fabric with the folded edge towards you. Hold the needle above the proposed hem and pointing diagonally, insert the needle just under the fold and pick up a couple of threads from the flat piece of face fabric, then bring the needle up through the hem diagonally. Repeat the process working to the left.

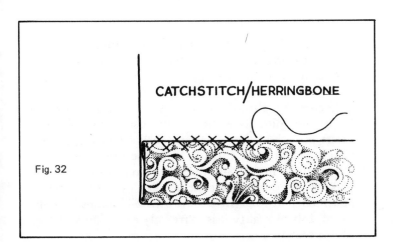

Fig. 32

Catchstitch

This stitch is also called herringbone, but current textbooks seem to have adopted the American name. It is useful for making unobtrusive hems on heavy fabrics where extra strength is necessary. It is also used to secure interlining to curtain fabric.

Work catchstitch from left to right on the wrong side of the fabric. Point your needle to the left. Take up a few threads from the flat layer of fabric and the folded fabric alternately. Keep the stitches as near the fold as possible. Repeat to produce a herringbone effect.

Oversewing

A simple way to neaten raw edges and prevent fraying. Working from left to right, take the needle through the fabric at an acute angle and draw the thread over the raw edge.

Slipstitch

The stitch you need to produce neat mitred corners

and apply lining to the main curtain fabric. It is used mostly to hold two folded edges of material together and is worked on the right side of the fabric from right to left.

Secure the thread as usual. Pick up a few threads from one fold, slide the needle inside the fold and insert into the other piece of fabric exactly opposite. Catch a couple of threads from the opposite fabric. Draw up the needle and thread and repeat the process. Make sure you re-insert the needle opposite the point at which you brought it out. This all sounds complicated, but in reality it is extremely easy. Look at Fig. 33 for reassurance.

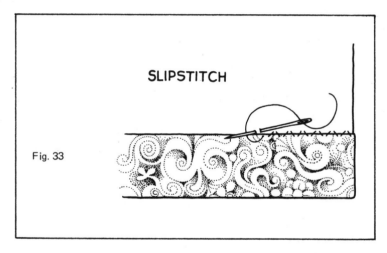

SLIPSTITCH

Fig. 33

Stabstitch

A simple stitch used to join two thick layers of fabric together.

Insert — or stab — your needle at right angles through the fabric and make your stitches approximately 0.5 cm long with equal spaces in between.

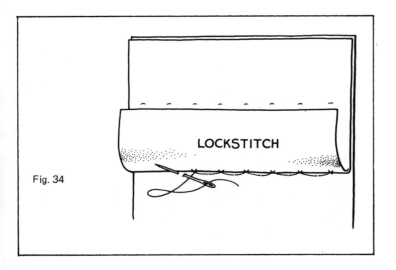

Fig. 34

LOCKSTITCH

Lockstitch

A loose stitch, approximately 1.2 cm long and worked from left to right down the length of a curtain, lockstitch is used exclusively to secure linings.

Seams

There are three basic types used to join widths of material together for curtains: the open seam, the flat run and fell seam and the French seam. By far the most commonly used is the simple flat seam, principally because it is unobtrusive. However, all three are easy to produce quite quickly with a sewing machine. Which you choose depends largely upon the strength of the seam required and the fabric used.

Basic Open Seam

With the raw edges together and the right sides facing, pin together the two pieces of fabric to be joined. Tack down the seam, removing the pins as you go.

Machine stitch *beside* the tacking line, making a few reverse stitches at both ends to give a firm finish.

→ Press the seam open. **At this point perfectionists neaten the edges with oversewing. Professional curtain makers rarely bother – except for materials which fray easily.**

The Run and Fell Seam

This seam gives a flatter finish than a French Seam. It is a particularly strong seam and thus very useful for unlined curtains.

Place the wrong sides of the fabric together with the raw edges even. Pin, tack and then machine approximately 1.5 cm from the edge. Press the seam open. Trim *one* edge to within about 0.5 cm of the sewing line. Turn in the other edge and fold this over the trimmed edge. Pin and then machine close to the fold or slipstitch by hand. Press.

French Seam

The French seam is the most suitable for joining together widths of net curtains. It is very hard-wearing and has the advantage that no lines of stitching show through on to the right side of the fabric.

Place the wrong sides of the fabric together with the raw edges even. Tack and stitch approximately 1 to 1.5 cm from the edge. Fabrics with a tendency to fray need the extra width.

Trim and remove the tacking. Turn the seam back on itself and stitch another seam 1 cm from the first, this time with the right sides together. Make sure you enclose the raw edges.

How to Mitre Corners

→ **Mitred corners are the professional way to achieve**

smooth, well-defined corners. A folded mitre is the method used to neaten fabric ends on lined and un-lined curtains. Contrast mitre is a technique used when applying a decorative braid border or braid.

The Folded Mitre

A truly perfect mitre can only be produced when the two hems are the same width. However, many curtain makers disregard this piece of theory, preferring to make the bottom hems slightly deeper (7.5 cm) than the side hems.

Here's the technique to use with equal hems. Adjust as necessary with uneven widths and look at Fig. 35(a) and (b) before you begin.

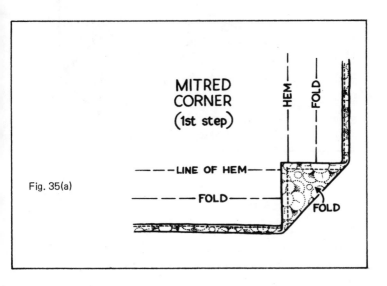

Fig. 35(a)

MITRED CORNER (1st step)

HEM
FOLD
LINE OF HEM
FOLD
FOLD

(a) Fold down the two hems so that they are of exactly equal width and press.

(b) Open the hems out flat and make sure the press

marks are clearly visible.

(c)   Fold the right side of the fabric over the wrong side, i.e., fold the corner inward on the inner fold lines. Press.

(d)   Cut off the corner, leaving a small seam allowance. Refold the hem to complete the mitre and slipstitch the two folds together.

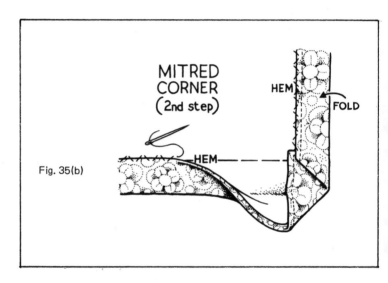

Fig. 35(b)

The Contrast Mitre

This sounds more complicated than it is.

(a)   Cut two lengths of decorative border – obviously, of equal width – and overlap them at right angles.

(b)   Fold under both ends of the border to make the mitre. Be sure to make your folds at an angle of 45 degrees. Press and tack into position.

(c)   Machine stitch along the tacked line on the wrong side. Trim away excess fabric and press.

Index